Engaging Men's Response to Family Violence / Andrew King
2017 Published by Groupwork Solutions
info@groupworksolutions.com.au
www.groupworksolutions.com.au

Print edition
ISBN: 978-0-6480015-0-8
Printed in Australia

Cover and interior design by Amie McCracken
Cover image from kasha_malasha

Images: Warren Porter
wporter@westnet.com.au

Sub editing: Steve Packer
stevepacker@ozemail.com.au

Engaging Men's Responses to Family Violence

a book of tools

Andrew King

Table of Contents

PREFACE

Reducing family violence has become a major focus in terms of community awareness, political will, media attention and everyday community services practice. Many current resources focus on supporting women and children, or the process of changing men's behaviour. This book is written from the point of view of a commentator reflecting on the context of behavioural change among men rather than that of an expert behaviour change specialist. It examines how community health/welfare/family support and counselling program workers can use a set of tools to engage male clients, and engage them enough that they access existing behaviour change resources. It is not an A-Z overview of family violence theory.

The book has a focus on early intervention and how workers can best respond to family violence issues and discussions with men before it becomes too dangerous. The largely gender-based nature of family violence needs to be acknowledged and valued to ensure victim safety. It should also be noted that this book has arisen from dialogues with practice experts who deal with family violence. Some of its wisdom has come from the context of men and family relationship services practice that occurred across Australia in the years 2000-2010. This context involved 56 programs (King, 2005) that engaged with men in their communities, with the aim of reducing family violence by building stronger family relationships.

It is sometimes asked 'why do you do this work and spend so much time in writing a book such as this'? My answer is that I want the world we live in to be a place where my daughters are safe from violence of all kinds. I admired the response of one of their boyfriends when his male friends challenged him to 'control his woman'. He said: "Firstly, she is not my woman. And secondly, I do not control her."

These messages about control and dominance are far more pervasive than the physical violence that is often associated with family abuse. Having tools that increase our confidence to deepen discussions with clients about control and family violence in relationships is vital for our society to flourish. The multisensory nature of the tools allows for the beliefs that someone has about their partner and children to be challenged without it being viewed personally as a confrontation.

The first section of the book explores a practice framework that provides community health/ welfare/ counselling and psychologist practitioners (referred to as workers) that unites the use of a feminist, strengths based and psychological tools required for working with men who use violence in intimate relationships. The second section provides ten tools for working with men that reduces their stuckness and increases their motivation towards positive change and accessing other support services.

It is important to remember, safety is always the core focus. Safety of the person experiencing violence, the children, yourself and the person who uses violence. Using the multisensory tools in this book is encouraged for low and moderate-risk situations, and with caution in medium-risk situations. They are never used in high-risk situations. In the end, safer relationships are created through insight with the likelihood that people will need to access further support.

1. THE EARLY INTERVENTION VISION

Society's best response to family violence is to create regular conversations that deepen wisdom and understanding in regard to the use of power and control in intimate relationships. These discussions need to explore people's understanding of family violence, along with the meaning of words such as 'entitlement' and 'privilege' and how these concepts are demonstrated in action. Its use is often so subtle that the effects are primarily unconscious and invisible to many people unless they are the ones who are disadvantaged by such experiences.

Early intervention is not about creating shame to demand action. It is focused on harnessing a person's ability to do something that is required of them, that is important and necessary. It is not about completing the whole process of behaviour change with the person, but eliciting an 'Ah-ha' moment when their own ethical understanding of their situation provides insight and motivation that they must act upon. With this increased motivation and purpose, they are more likely to use other behaviour change resources that are available to them.

This book explores a wide range of viewpoints and experiences workers encounter when dealing with men and family relationships. It is intended to supplement other family violence readings rather than cover all the issues in comprehensive depth and detail. It is vital that workers can make informed referrals to local behaviour change programs. It is very useful to know about their intake processes and who is likely to be involved. Giving male clients the names of the intake workers they need to speak to increases the likelihood that they will make initial contact.

It is argued here that feminist, psychological approaches and strengths-based interventions can be used together without undermining the traditional gendered understanding of family violence. The feminist approach has provided a significant platform for greater gender equity throughout society in a change process that is still far from complete.

All violence in family relationships is unacceptable, and the most important issue is the effect it has on the victims, including the children. When children are repeatedly exposed or subjected to violence, another generation of violence is being incubated. The issue of safety is fundamental to working on cases of family violence and it is critical that workers never underplay this concern.

Feminist theories now argue that family violence has a wide range of causes. Men's behaviour can be understood through the impact of a male privilege/entitlement belief system, and through using a psychological emphasis regarding the impact of trauma or negative social learning. Both perspectives are vital and one should not compromise the significance of the other. In fact, it can be argued that social learning and other psychological approaches are supported by feminist practice (DeKeseredy & Dragiewicz, 2007).

Family violence work needs to:

- Retain the need to ensure safety for all.
- Challenge belief systems and focus on privilege/entitlement.
- Work for wider social change because these beliefs are widespread throughout all levels of society.

However, when working with clients, an integration of psychological (Heise, 1998; DeKeseredy & Dragiewicz, 2007) and strengths-based approaches is required, as long as safety issues are not compromised.

Generativity, defined as concern for establishing and guiding the next generation, is a key framework for the tools in this book. It utilises life stages of development to enhance motivation for change and purpose. The generative framework is best captured in men's roles and responsibilities as a parent. In that context, a father's capacity to support change is increased. The worker uses the challenge that arises between the hopes and aspirations of a father and the starkly conflicting threat of violence. With clients who aren't fathers, another generative connection needs to be identified and explored (see chapter 6).

The tools used are multisensory and are best understood in the tradition of Impact Therapy. This brief form of therapy draws from existing theories such as Rational Emotive Therapy, Transactional Analysis and Gestalt. Its use is compatible with systems theory, Adlerian counselling, Reality Therapy and most other theories. Impact Therapy is action and insight oriented, and often resolution oriented. It emphasises helping the client as much as possible (Jacobs & Schimmel, 2013) and is best appreciated through the four M's:

The four M's of Impact Therapy

Multisensory	Using multisensory tools activates the neurons in the brain, which tends to make the session more effective and increase meaning attribution and recall at a later date. The brain likes novelty, so it is important to 'speak to the eyes, not just the ears'. Multisensory tools include props, paper, butchers paper, chairs, mindfulness and experiential learning exercises.
Motivational	Working with clients' needs to increase their motivation. This is best achieved by focusing on the balance of desire/aspiration and challenge/fear/blocks that get in the way. Workers need to regularly ask themselves if the session is leading to a new and deeper level of understanding for the shared purpose.
Marketing	Marketing is about creating the relevance in our work to what the client needs. Many clients don't immediately identify the relevance. They need to see that other community supports are going to be an opportunity to do something different rather than a hassle or boring experience.
Maps	As you might expect, maps are tools workers use to help enable clients to get to where they need to go. They are the psychological and sociological frameworks we are trained to use. Key maps are rational emotive behaviour therapy and mindfulness.

Table 1: The 4 M's workers utilize

The tools are not intended to be used in any specific order. Workers need to assess for themselves which to use first, and subsequently. It is not intended that this engagement process involves the whole behaviour change process. The use of the tools is to increase awareness and motivation (through developing an 'Ah-ha' moment of insight), so the client is more likely to act on a referral to access a behaviour change program.

To gain the most from reading this book, it is good to think about a likely situation you will face in your work that conforms to the following conditions. If you don't work with fathers, choose a typical male client you are likely to work with.

A typical family violence situation

Write down a situation involving family violence that has or could occur in your work (not necessarily the worst or easiest to deal with). Do **not** include how you dealt with the context.

- What is the father's hypothetical name?

- Who else is involved (other key family members)?

- What are the key background issues?

- What has just happened?

The tools use a relationship-rich focus to support change. When working with men, effective language involves three key components as illustrated in Figure 1. These components are used in the context of your work relationships and within a workplace safety framework that promotes safe work practice. For example, each organisation has policies about workplace safety practices when providing after-hours counselling services.

Most policies are developed with reference to such core components, making them relevant to the development of male-friendly language. The core components for the skills workers use to improve engagement are:

Workplace Safety

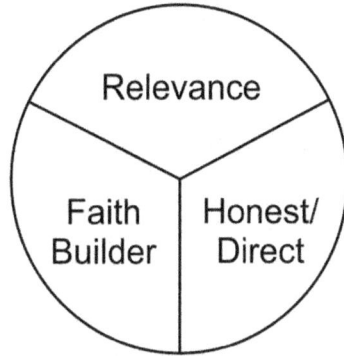

Figure 1: Key worker engagement skills

- Relevance – the discussion needs to be relevant to the client's needs.
- Faith building – the worker needs to convey the belief that the man has the ability to commit, choose, care, change, create, connect and communicate.
- Honest/direct – most male clients respect people who honestly and respectfully discuss with them the important issues in their life.

These engagement skills are best captured in the concept of straight-talking. This involves:

- Providing a context and reason to have the discussion.
- Validating the impact of the issues being discussed.
- Describing the issues and concerns in specific, concrete terms.
- Enquiring into and acknowledging people's efforts and intentions.
- Acknowledging strengths and exceptions.
- Checking for constraints (anything else that gets in the way).
- Identifying specifically what needs to be different.
- Describing steps that need to be completed.

Additional skills workers use (Jenkins, 2009) when working with men and they have the informed consent of the client and their partner (preferred if possible) include:

A. Establishing trust

- Create a safe, respectful and honest environment.

- Allow them to move at their own pace.
- Ask permission to explore certain avenues before doing so.
- Be sensitive to their shame and guilt.
- Work to get acknowledgment of the violence once communication is established.

B. Acknowledgement

- Once there is an acknowledgement of violent/abusive/controlling behaviour:

  o Listen carefully to their language/cognitive processes;
  o Use their language initially;
  o Acknowledge their courage in talking about difficult issues; and
  o Use language that is non-judgmental.

C. Tracking behaviour

- Get clear and accurate description of their behaviour – frequency, length of time in the relationship, seriousness and escalation patterns.
- Introduce the notion of a cycle of violence. Where are they in the cycle?
- Track their beliefs about being in control.

D. Exploring

- Explore their awareness of the impact of their behaviour.
- What is the impact on their partner, children, self?
- What is level of empathy for partner/family?
- What legacy do they want to leave their children?
- Are the children frightened of them? What impact does this have on the children?
- Explore their readiness/willingness to change their behaviour.
- Notice responsibility avoidance language – denial, minimisation, blaming, justification.
- Discuss powerlessness and not taking responsibility.
- Link taking responsibility and their reasons for wanting something to change. What do they want to change now?
- Explore their perceived benefits and downsides (long term/short term) of their behaviour.

- Discuss how the violence/abuse must stop before other relationship issues can be addressed.

E. Safety of partner and children

- Explore immediate and long-term safety of partner and children.
- Discuss safety plans and strategies.
- Seek co-operation in keeping partner safe. What can they do?
- Provide the men with anger management strategies e.g. time-out.
- Provide them with referral or direct link to family violence services in their locality.
- Assist them to explore how the violence is affecting their partner's and children's life.

All family violence practice holds safety as a central focus. This most often involves ensuring that the victims of violence, often the women and children, are safe. It is useful to review the situation using a risk assessment tool.

Risk assessment guide (GCDVIP, 2014)

Using the multisensory tools in this book is encouraged for low and moderate-risk situations, and with caution in medium-risk situations. They are never used in high-risk situations.

In assessing risk the following factors are also considered: mental health state, type of Domestic Violence Order (DVO/ AVO) he might have in place, previous breach of these orders, access to fire-arms, his potential unem-

Violent behaviour may be linked with, concealing or complicated by other issues. Professionals need to look out for and be sensitive to any cues that indicate:

- Ongoing conflict or arguments
- Poor communication
- Virulent criticism of the partner
- Withdrawal of sexual relations by partner
- A departure from the house
- Jealous and antagonist responses to any new relationship that the partner may have
- An Intervention Order or Apprehended Violence Order (AVO).

ployment, his use of violence (particularly if a partner is pregnant) and any past or present use of choking.

HIGH RISK

1. An incident reported in previous week and possibility of threats suggested.
2. Clear inconsistencies with worker's perceptions, information supplied by partner or other sources.
3. Imminent change in situational factors signalled or suggested as being of concern (e.g. separation, reconciliation, change in contact).

Important responses to people who use violence:

- Identify violence and control issues in the relationship.
- Assess the immediate/short-term level of risk.
- Assist them to gain an understanding of the impact of their behaviour e.g. "How does it feel to know that your partner and kids were afraid of you last night?"
- Engage the person so they begin to take responsibility for their behaviour.
- Refer or link them to behaviour change programs and family violence support services.

4. The person who uses violence discloses suicidal/self-harm thoughts or plans.
5. Concern over conceptual understanding, safety strategies, position-taking on non-violence.
6. Continued high levels of denial, minimisation and blame.
7. If the potential for violence exists, the police must be informed.

MEDIUM RISK

1. An incident reported in previous week and possibility of threats suggested.
2. Some clear inconsistencies with workers' perceptions, information supplied by partner or other sources.
3. Possibility of change in situational factors signalled or suggested as being of current concern.

4. Limited evidence of conceptual understanding and position-taking on non-violence.
5. The person who uses violence continues to use denial, minimisation and blame.
6. Some safety strategies articulated, but limited demonstration.
7. Follow-up required during next week to clarify risk concerns and to discuss appropriate safety responses with the participant, partner and other relevant agencies. Contact with female partner. Police involvement may be required.

MODERATE RISK

1. No violent incident in previous week or threats suggested.
2. Some inconsistencies with workers' perceptions, information supplied by partner or other sources.
3. No change in situational factors signalled or suggested as being of current concern.
4. Some evidence of conceptual understanding and position-taking on non-violence
5. The person who uses violence shows some use of denial, minimisation and blame.
6. Some safety strategies developed and demonstrated.
7. No immediate action required at present. Monitor any change next week. Maintain contact with female partner.

LOW RISK

1. No violent incident in previous week or threats suggested.
2. Information consistent with workers' perceptions and that supplied by partner/other sources.
3. No change in situational factors signalled or suggested as being of concern.
4. Evidence of clear conceptual understanding and position-taking on non-violence.
5. The person who uses violence shows no evidence of denial, minimisation or blame.

6. Safety strategies developed and demonstrated.
7. No immediate action required.

Engaging men in behaviour change

The following checklist (Cooke, 2006) has useful pointers for workers to be conscious of when working with family violence. It mirrors the wisdom used by behaviour change workers:

- The central focus of family violence is psychological and emotional abuse that involves patterns of control and coercion, not just physical violence. Many women have been socially conditioned to privilege male voices above their own. The purpose of men's behaviour change is to keep women and children safe.
- A good introduction to new male clients: "If you have been given this info, you are probably feeling uncomfortable. You will have a few things to think about."
- Don't view the men as powerless. They are social change agents. Always hold the view that men using abuse and violence have the capability and competency to change and that the use of any violence is a choice.
- Men with misogynist attitudes may not use abuse but will support other men's abuse.
- Men choosing abuse need to be connected to choices. They are not powerless. Take them back to the beginnings of their relationship. They would have rarely used violence at the beginning of the relationship as their partner would have left them.
- Men are not always abusive. Violence is probably not something that the man uses in other contexts, or not to this extent. He also had a period of non-abuse at beginning of relationship. It is about enacting and sustaining control, not loss of control.
- Always tell men what you are going to do before you do it. Remind them that you said earlier on you that you are going to challenge their beliefs. "Is that okay? Are you ready for it?"

- Goal setting is essential. Review every six weeks.
- Think about the underlying theories you use in your work. These theories will affect your approach to the interventions you use. What would women say about your theory?
- Female feedback is essential.
- Too much focus on relationship theory can lead us to victim blaming and isn't helpful to men's behaviour change.
- Avoid too much curiosity in trying to work the man out. It is about choice and change.
- Avoid boundaries of the program becoming blurred e.g. accepting lateness, delving into 'he said, she said'.
- Avoid going down the rabbit hole of explanations. Focus on the experience, not the explanation. Men know they are being abusive. Don't encourage them to assume powerlessness in that they don't know what abuse is.
- If the focus shifts to blame or 'he said, she said', return to his child or children's perspective.
- Look for the women's responses to the violence. This resistance speaks to their resilience. "If you don't have a description of the resistance, you don't have a complete description of the violence. It colludes with the offender If you omit responses."
  – Alan Wade (Wade, 2015)

2. Overview of Family Violence

Family violence is a complex issue that professional counsellors, health and community welfare workers will encounter when working with men. Many men accessing programs will either talk about their own use of violence, or their potential for it. They may also want to discuss episodes of violence committed against them.

In the community, many people argue about the validity of a gendered or non-gendered understanding of family violence.

It is important for workers to be able to explain the meaning of family violence without the use of technical language or a statistical debate.

> A good metaphor for family violence is the umbrella, with its central pole representing homicide – the murder of women in intimate relationships. The pole only accounts for a small part of the umbrella. The canopy is vital and represents the breadth of family violence issues – physical, psychological, financial, sexual, intimidation, the use of children, etc.

Most definitions of family violence are similar to this: "Behaviour within a domestic relationship that involves an abuse of power and is usually, though not exclusively, perpetrated by men against women and children. Family violence encompasses a range of behaviours including intimidation, coercion, emotional abuse, financial abuse, sexual abuse, physical abuse, isolation and psychological manipulation." (Mulroney, 2002, p. 3).

There is increasing evidence that the influence of male privilege exists on a continuum and depends on each man's background (family history, education, lived experience in regard to work/peers/relationships).

> "Violence is defined broadly as any attempt to influence, coerce or control another person where there is potential to cause harm, violate the integrity of the other or disrespect the other's differences." (Jenkins, 2009, p. 3)

Violence is clearly not confined within a select, psychologically disturbed or deviant group of individuals. We all can, and at times do, enact violence which causes offence or harm to others. Much of this violence is enacted with a sense of entitlement and sense of justification, and follows a common formula:

- Sense of affront or outrage: *"How dare you...!"*
- Desire to be correct: *"I'll show you!"*
- Corrective or punitive action: *"Take that!"*
- Attribution or responsibility: *"You deserve it!"*
- Entitled sense of justification: *"Now don't do it again!"* (Jenkins, 2009)

Violence has the potential to be abusive when the person who enacts it:

- Possesses a significant advantage or privilege in relation to the other due to factors that confer power, such as age, strength, ability or conferred status.
- Experiences an exaggerated (and generally ongoing) sense of entitlement in relation to the other, thereby justifying its use.
- Abdicates responsibility for the well-being of the other (generally on an ongoing basis) and thereby justifies or excuses its harmful consequences. (Jenkins, 2009)

All coercion has the potential to cause harm. But not all forms do produce harmful violation or lead to the disrespect of individuals, particularly when the coercion is enacted within an accountable context where the potential is considered, and the nature and effects of coercive action are carefully monitored (Jenkins, 2009).

A significant amount of family violence behaviour is a premeditated attempt to coerce or control a partner, while other behaviours are influenced by other reactive elements, such as attachment anxiety (Sutton, 2007b; Dutton, 2008). However, control and power tactics are often not premeditated or even conscious, and much of the work that needs to be done is about making the unconscious conscious.

Table 2: Tactics used by people who use violence against their partner

Physical violence	Punching, hitting, slapping, shoving, throwing objects, pulling hair, twisting limbs, choking.
Sexual assault	Sexual intercourse or other sexual acts without consent, unwanted sexual touching.
Use of weapons	Guns and other weapons used directly or threatened to be used.
Psychological and emotional abuse	Regular putdowns, name-calling, threatening to harm adults or children, threats of suicide. These actions destroy a person's sense of self-esteem and distort their perception and right to be safe and free from abuse.
Intimidation	Intimidating or frightening someone, injuring or destroying pets, throwing items that may just miss a person, damaging property.
Stalking	Following the woman about, waiting outside her home or place of work.
Social isolation and abuse	Isolating the woman from family and friends, not allowing her outside, preventing her from leaving the home and accessing transportation, restricting her use of the telephone, controlling who she sees and where she goes, humiliating her in public.
Financial abuse	Preventing the woman from accessing financial resources, not allowing her to have her own bank account, demanding that she hand over any income she obtains, depriving her or her children of basic physical needs.

One practice issue is that it is important to 'put words to deeds'. In the working stage with clients, and maybe less in the engagement stage, it is important to describe behaviours with appropriate language.

In Figure 2, the continuum highlights some of the behaviours in the violence spectrum.

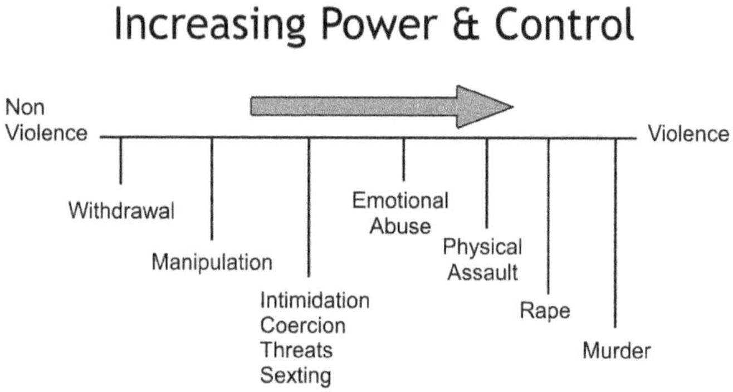

Increasing Power & Control

Figure 2: Spectrum of violent behaviours

The Australian Personal Safety Survey (2012) that acknowledged that one in six women (16.9 per cent) and about one in nineteen men (5.3 per cent) experienced at least one incident of physical or sexual violence in a lifetime (ABS, 2013). However, these figures should not be misused. The survey indicated that the violence experienced by men and women was mostly perpetrated by men. The survey enquired about acts experienced and did not explore the context or meaning of the violence. Reflecting on previous surveys, "interviews with the same men and women documented that men's violence differed systematically from women's in terms of its nature, frequency, intention, intensity, physical injury and emotional impact." (Flood, 2006). This is consistent with international research (DeKeseredy & Dragiewicz, 2007; Dobash & Dobash, 2004).

One of the current tensions in practice is that, as more men access community welfare/health and relationship programs, there is a greater voice for their experience regarding violence. This experience needs to be heard and acknowledged, but the hearing of this voice at the individual level can't cease to be informed by the wider context of violence as experienced in the community.

Family violence occurs in marriages, defacto relationships, between boyfriends and girlfriends, in gay and lesbian relationships, and between family members. In the overwhelming majority of cases (95%), it is the male who abuses his female partner or ex-partner. (Mulroney, 2002)

Traditionally, family violence is seen within sociocultural/political theories (feminist and functionalist theories) where family violence is a consequence of the structural inequality and patriarchal privilege between men and women. The majority of injuries, deaths and negative outcomes that result from family violence occur to women. From this perspective, men's violence is usually in a context where men have more power, either physically or due to their privileged opportunities in our society. While there is now documentation of violence that women perpetrate against men, the amount of violence by men against women is also underreported.

There are various ideas about the range of behaviours that fall under the category of 'violence'. People commonly think of physical acts when they think of violence. The judicial system has legal definitions that include verbal threats and intimidation, but stop short of the subtler forms of control and abuse. The exception is Victoria, where new laws now prevent non-physical forms of family violence such as financial abuse. Most family violence agencies, including those with programs for people who perpetrate violence, consider behaviours such as the 'silent treatment', put-downs and keeping secrets as important to name as controlling acts.

The effects of family violence on women include (Mulroney, 2002):

- Feelings of worthlessness and low self-esteem.
- Physical and emotional exhaustion.
- Anxiety and hyper-vigilance.
- Feeling responsible for their partner's actions.
- Blaming themselves.
- Health problems associated with poor wellbeing.
- Mental minimisation of the effects of the abuse on themselves and the children.

- Self-doubt and difficulty in making decisions.
- Depression.
- Higher rates of attempted suicide.
- High rates of drug and alcohol abuse.
- Increased likelihood of abusing dependent children.

Children often feel isolated and have no power to stop the violence. The effects of the violence remain with them throughout their lifetime, and similar patterns can occur in their adult relationships. Children suffer significant negative effects as a result of domestic violence. Domestic violence can be experienced in a number of ways (Mulroney, 2002):

- Being direct targets of abuse.
- Witnessing violence perpetrated against a parent (usually the mother).
- Being in another room and hearing violence occurring.
- Being physically assaulted while trying to protect their parent (usually the mother).
- Living in a household filled with constant tension and fear.

The effects of domestic violence on children include:

- Aggressive behaviour and acting out
- Self-blame
- Depression
- Bed-wetting
- Difficulty relating to peers
- Running away
- Poor concentration
- Drug and alcohol problems
- Depression and anxiety
- Over-compliance
- Pseudo-maturity.

3. Development of an Integrated Framework

It is sad when three important frameworks for working with men (feminist, psychological and strengths-based) are polarised against each other. Recognising that these frameworks are used widely, workers will experience tensions or challenges when applying them to working with men and violence issues. There are current developments within feminist theory and from other perspectives to create a more unified framework. (Heise, 1998)

There appears to be a current paradigm debate regarding family violence causes and interventions that may make it difficult for workers to develop a clear, coherent and consistent big picture (Sutton, 2007b). This occurs as people use different paradigms to think about their work practice. The abuse paradigm uses socio-cultural/socio-political approach theories to focus on explaining family violence through the patriarchal beliefs of male entitlement (learned by men as they grow up and influenced by the way their society/culture is structured). The conflict paradigm uses psychological, relationship and strengths-based approaches to provide opportunities for change. Both perspectives are vital and can't operate in isolation.

Conflict	Abuse
No fault divorce	DV framework
Child focussed	Crime/Legal sanction
Use of community studies of violence	Use of State Court crime statistics
Argue for symmetry gender experiences for violence	Asymmetrical approach to violence. Worried about unintended consequences

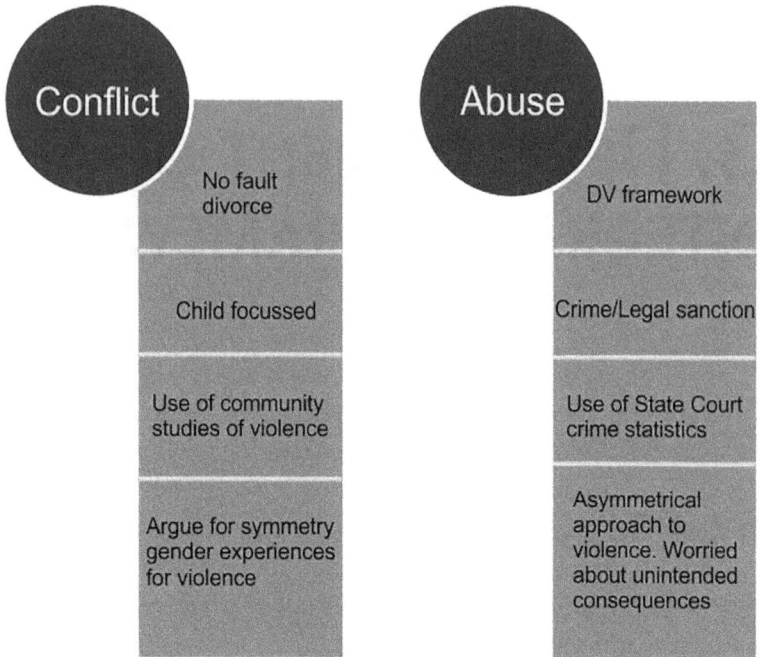

Figure 3: Overview of some key positions associated with the conflict and abuse paradigms

Heise (1998) advocates for a joint framework that holds together psychological, sociological, criminological and feminist perspectives. Often the interconnection of these frameworks is avoided due to fear that one framework will dominate the other. This is an ongoing risk and, in a practice context, it is worked with and minimised daily.

Heise states that "although theories based on stress, social learning and personality disorders may suggest why individual men become violent, they do not explain why women are so persistently the target" (Heise, 1998). To work with the tensions, she advocated for the ecological framework below (Figure 4) that recognises the interconnection of the personal experience, microsystems, exosystems (the system between the individual and broader social experience) and macrosystems.

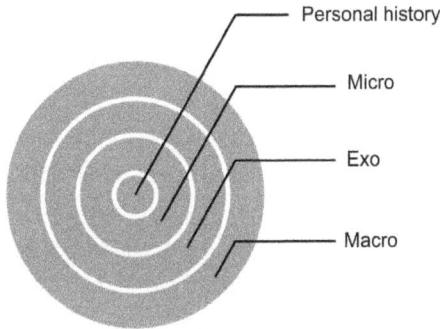

Figure 4: Heise's Ecological Framework

Personal history

- Experiencing family violence as a child.
- Being abused as a child.
- Impact of absent or rejecting role models.

Microsystem

- Male dominance in the family.
- Male control of wealth in the family.
- Use of alcohol.
- Marital/verbal conflict.

Exosystem

- Low socioeconomic status/unemployment.
- Isolation of women and the family.
- Delinquent peer associations.

Macrosystem

- Belief in male entitlement/ownership of women.
- Masculinity linked to aggression and dominance.
- Rigid gender roles.
- Acceptance of interpersonal violence. (Heise, 1998)

Heise's framework holds together the political analysis and the individual focus as used by Dutton, Sonkin and others. The psychological approach adds another layer to working with family violence and men. A new, emerging psychological approach is neurobiology where many parts of the brain are involved in processing information and thinking, not just the cerebral cortex. It is now known that the limbic system also does much of our 'thinking', often at an automatic and unconscious level, because it is processing multiple levels of feelings. There are also brain structures whose role is to integrate these two systems so they can function together in an integrated way (Sutton, 2007b).

It is also now known that early socioemotional attachment determines how well this processing develops, and what developmental deficits will determine 'affect regulation' deficits that will contribute to anger or violence in later life (Sutton, 2007b). Thus, if certain emotions are regularly experienced in early childhood, this will influence a person's cognitive beliefs. To work with this, workers examine whether effective interventions respond to 'affect regulation' deficits at the emotional level and not just at the analytical cognitive level (Sutton, 2007b). As the integration of this perspective is applied to family violence work with men, the lessons learnt through the feminist approach remains a central foundation, with the primary focus being the safety of the whole family.

Strengths-based practice has been a foundation in many community and relationship programs. Strengths-based practice views people as having sufficient resources and strengths to meet their challenges and problems with new solutions, until proven otherwise. Through using these existing resources to respond to change, it allows workers to engage with a wider range of people with a greater capacity for change. It also allows the worker to challenge the men to an even deeper level about attitudes, beliefs and what change is required, without them becoming defensive or even aggressive. The strengths-based approach provides one of the strongest containers to talk about significant problems and challenges, and explore possible solutions.

The worker ensures specific safety issues and behaviours are named and confronted through the use of straight-talking (see Chapter 1). The use of a strengths-based framework remains continually informed by the use of feminist frameworks and psychological interventions such as Cognitive Behavioural Therapy (CBT), Rational Emotive Behaviour Therapy and 'affect regulation', with the primary focus remaining on assuring safety.

Professionals working with men and families need to remember the following:

- Safety of all involved in any intervention is the first and primary consideration.
- No information obtained from the victim is passed on to the person who uses violence.
- This work requires a careful balance of engaging the man around his use of violence, while avoiding collusion.
- The physical and economic power imbalance that often exists between men and women.
- All violence in relationships is unacceptable.
- Children witnessing family violence are traumatised and affected emotionally and psychologically for life, thus creating another adult generation that uses these behaviours.
- Accountability practices involve having the victims' stories in mind while working with men or women.

4. SUPPORTING BEHAVIOUR CHANGE WITH PEOPLE WHO USE VIOLENCE

Characteristics of men who use violence

It is difficult to provide one typography of people who use violence. Feminist theory has been "deeply committed to enhancing a rich empirical and theoretical understanding of women's use of violence" (DeKeseredy & Dragiewicz, 2007). Other contexts have endeavoured to better understand the different shades and expressions of family violence.

Michael Johnson, who was Associate Professor of Sociology, Women's Studies, and African and African-American Studies at Pennsylvania State University, in the US, is often positively referred to by both the abuse and conflict paradigm writers. He identified family violence as having four different contexts:

- In *intimate terrorism* or *coercive violence*, the individual is violent and controlling, the partner is not. It is primarily gendered, with men being the prime users of this motivation. The violence is usually severe and it tends to escalate, and injuries are common. Evidence indicates that men are more likely than women to use this type of violence in family relationships and it is likely to result in far greater injury towards women (Dobash & Dobash, 2004). It is a highly gendered form of family violence. It is this spectrum of behaviour that informs a lot of family violence research.
- In *conflict-instigated violence* or *situational couple violence*, although the individual is violent, the behaviour is reac-

tionary due to emotional overload or extreme stress, rather than deliberately controlling. "Here the violence is relatively minor, both partners practice it, is expressive in meaning, it tends not to escalate over time and injuries are rare." (Flood, 2006).

- In *violent resistance*, the partner who regularly experiences violence reacts with violence (an act of self-preservation, a justifiable response when one's human rights are violated). Some people argue that it is unfair and inappropriate to refer to these behaviours as violence as they are motivated by self-defence or the protection of others. Predominantly it is women who use this violence as a backlash or in self-defence. When cases go before the courts, it is often questioned if this response should be seen as violence.

- In *separation-instigated violence*, both partners can be violent and controlling. Johnson (2007) explores evidence that situational couple violence dominates in general surveys (of large sample size) while intimate terrorism and violent resistance dominate in court-based studies (smaller sample size). It describes violence instigated by separation where there was no prior history in the intimate partner relationship or in other settings. It involves unexpected and uncharacteristic acts of violence perpetrated by a partner with a history of civilised and contained behaviour. The partner who has been left is more likely to use this violence.

Even though the identification of the differences between these motivations is difficult to gauge, our sector's understanding of family violence requires better articulation of the differences Johnson has described. Johnson's categories are valued by the sector, but they have been criticised because real case scenarios cannot be allocated where:

- Cases don't fit.
- Multiple motivations exist.
- Reliable assessment instruments don't fit.
- False negatives and positives occur.

There is value in further researching the different types of family violence, although in reality these types probably exist on overlapping continuums rather than as discreet categories. The most significant criticism is that motivation and use of violence is difficult for someone else to judge as it is regularly downplayed or underreported, and incorrect use of classification may lead to victims of violence being at greater risk.

Recent developments in service provision have identified that there can be a hierarchy within the worker-client relationship in which the counsellor can assume a position of superiority. This can be seen as perpetuating the model already embraced by those using violence, rather than providing choices through modelling alternative behaviour. A big challenge for a worker is to become aware of his/her own 'capacity to abuse their power'; that is, the worker's desire to force learning on someone else. It is critical for workers to access regular supervision and to cultivate an awareness of their own attitudes and habitual ways of being. It is important to avoid totalising views of men e.g. defining them only as users of violence. Language such as 'perpetrator' or 'predator' encourages this totalising.

> "Perhaps the most significant consolidation in invitational theory and practice is the notion of the parallel journey for workers. This concept refers to understandings of the political nature of intervention and the belief that our journeys as workers must mirror the journeys of our clients." (Jenkins, 2009, p. xiii)

Having this one-dimensional, deficiency-based view of a person will restrict the change process. When the violence occurs in a current relationship, a better term to use is 'person who uses violence' or 'person concerned about their use of violence'. In behaviour change programs, it is essential to provide ongoing support and contact as well as confidential follow-up with the (ex) partners of the men. This is a safety mechanism and maintains accountably to the victims of violence. With this in mind, the worker is working for both the person who uses violence and their victims.

Jenkins highlights the importance of building on the underlying ethical framework that most people use. "Becoming ethical is contrasted with being violent, being respectful of people's actions, etc. The latter focus can fail to open up new possibilities for becoming ethical. This position is not based on any humanistic notion, or basic goodness within people, or basic externally prescribed moral standards, but on the productive concepts of life and desire, as proposed by Deleuze, which "point to ethics which are immanent to the striving notions of individuals and communities to engage with life" (Jenkins, 2009, p. xii).

> "Invitational practice places considerable focus upon the clarification and repositioning of the experience of shame from a context which is disabling (restrictive) and debilitating, to one which is enabling and which signifies integrity and promotes ethical ways forward." (Jenkins, 2009, p. xiii)

The ongoing victim support and evaluation process can be difficult to maintain as it is time-intensive and partners may have hesitation in being involved. It is not appropriate to work with men on family violence unless the safety, support and accountability processes are operating and integrated. Female workers are critical to this work, regardless of the challenge to create the initial safety for men to speak truthfully and build sufficient trust. Female workers are often seen as a valuable source of knowledge by providing a woman's perspective.

Historical development of family violence programs for men

MBC programs began largely in the United States and have been running for about 20 years. Other English-speaking western countries such as Great Britain, Canada, Australia and New Zealand have set up similar programs. The Adelaide Domestic Violence Service began one of the first programs in the late 1980s for men who were troubled by their violence. (Sutton, 2007b)

• Social learning models

Initially, the first group interventions were based on social learning theory which proposes that social behaviours are learnt in early childhood and that learnt behaviours are maintained by various reinforcing events and social beliefs. These groups therefore focused on behavioural change in dealing with stressful emotions and situations (especially anger management). 'Skill deficit' models proposed that anger and violence was a result of skill deficits such as low frustration tolerance, lack/loss of control, learned helplessness, etc. These formed the basis for the well-known 'cycle of violence' models. (Sutton, 2007b)

• Cognitive behavioural therapy interventions (CBT)

Following social learning theory, CBT interventions were designed to change dysfunctional learned behaviour by cognitive restructuring of 'irrational' thinking and emotions, along with skill development.

A major CBT goal is increased self-observation, which is facilitated by self-monitoring via 'anger logs' that record and analyse stressful situations and incidents. This helps users of violence to learn to identify their triggers, self-talk and consequences. The ability to stop and question their impulsive internal dialogues is regularly reported by many men to be the single most effective skill they learn in group programs. (Sutton, 2007b)

• 'Feminist' sociocultural models

Feminism is not a therapy model as such, but a set of beliefs and structures that give priority to a feminist analysis of gender and power in relationships and society. Feminist analysis focuses on external systems such as patriarchal structures and sexist practices that shape the social construction of gender. Gender role socialisation results in rigid sex roles based on male privilege and entitlement that lead to unreasonable and unfair expectations of women and a lack of empathy and consideration for their needs, feelings, beliefs and values. (Sutton, 2007b)

The feminist approach is widely adopted, especially with increasing awareness of family violence and its impact on children. However, it recognises that multiple perspectives are required to work with family violence as long as the safety issues are not impacted. Feminism is often inaccurately polarised in the debate as being too simplistic or only focusing on structural analysis of society. With the feminist traditions are many viewpoints. Feminist writers have recently embarked on exploring the accumulating evidence of significant violence and abuse in gay and lesbian relationships. "While the concepts of gender and patriarchy are useful to account for the huge incidence of violence against women, feminist theories should not become a 'regime of truth' that is applied to all individual cases of violence. We need a more complex approach – one that sees power as a relational dynamic and recognises sexuality, culture, class, race, age and ability as well as gender." (McKenzie, 2003; Gondolf, 2007)

As a worker, the debate between feminist and psychological approaches to change behaviour has an endless range of perspectives. Some of the tensions that exist:

- Behaviour change programs fundamentally work to change beliefs about the tactics of power and control in a patriarchal society rather than use psychological methods like CBT to change behavior.
- Gondolf, a strong pro-feminist researcher, advocates for the Duluth Behaviour Change Model, which is based on CBT and community development approaches. He strongly advocates for the use of guilt and shame as tools for change because men who use violence are seen as likely to feel little guilt and more likely to blame others for their behaviour. "Obviously, scolding or condemning individuals is not what Duluth promotes, but confronting men's behaviour in a more systemic way does have some justification." (Gondolf, 2007)
- All group interventions are viewed as being 'psychoeducational', or about re-education regarding power/control rather

than the use of a 'therapeutic' or psychological approach that may individualise the cause of the violence, and may excuse men's behaviour and therefore limit them from taking responsibility for their actions.

• Skill-based models such as anger management are seen as neglecting to address the violence against women and children because these programs fail to name and expose the tactics of power and control, and are often the easier and shorter programs for men to access. Anger is often managed well by people who use violence, with the rewards being more based on the beliefs about others and the benefits of controlling them.

The future development of behaviour change programs requires embracing the feminist specific and the best use of psychological and strengths-based approaches to create change. Johnson (2007) has found that not all violence is motivated by patriarchal privilege. According to him, some family violence occurs when men feel powerless and without a voice. However, a man may feel powerless because his sense of entitlement is not being acknowledged.

No matter what the motivation, violence is unacceptable. Alan Jenkins, an Australian psychologist and family violence worker, developed an approach based on narrative therapy called 'invitations to responsibility'. Jenkins supports men to make an ethical stand against their abusive behaviour by encouraging them to take responsibility for it and provide direction on how to act with respect and care (Jenkins, 1993). Using this respectful approach allows a practitioner to work with men to take responsibility while using a strengths-based approach i.e. narrative therapy.

Working with men to change family violence behaviours

Although there are problems with the concept of anger management, many men relate to it and are motivated to attend such group programs. This is because men are usually not looking for 'affect regulation'; they are looking for 'effect regulation' – or tighter control of their behaviour that follows emotional arousal. Historically, usually this is promoted by feedback from key people in their life or authorities such as the police or court system.

However, current professional understanding is moving in the direction of seeing effective anger management as helping men to proactively deal more effectively with all of their emotions, rather than learn how to control their anger. Men are often referred by other professionals for anger management as if it is a quick-fix, one-size-fits-all magic wand solution (Sutton, 2007a). This is highlighted in media reports where public figures, such as Sam Newman (retired Australian rules football player), have been mandated to undergo counselling for anger management issues, further blurring distinctions between self-regulation and punitive action. It is critical that professionals understand that the solution involves more comprehensive affect regulation and that individuals require quite different periods of intervention for behaviour change to be successful (Sutton, 2007a).

Another reason men relate to the idea of anger management is because it's okay to feel and act angry, because it doesn't challenge the male stereotype, whereas showing other emotions is seen as feminine. It is therefore not problematic (threatening) for men to sit in a group and articulate their 'problems with anger' and it often takes some time to move the discussion to other emotions. It is also recognised that it is difficult for men to access these services in many rural areas.

The term anger management is problematic in the eyes of various professionals/services because it is often erroneously used interchangeably with the concept of a MBC group program (Sutton, 2007a). This is problematic because it blurs the distinction between emotional responses and the sociocultural and gender issues that support family violence (e.g. power and control). While it is generally accepted to have anger management or affect regulation groups for men who have problematic low levels of 'anger', some of the behaviour management strategies used in affect regulation programs are similar to those found in MBC group programs (Sutton, 2007a). However, while some strategies overlap, each context uses very different underpinning framework and philosophy.

It is important that workers refer men to the most appropriate programs and that anger management is not seen as an alternative to being involved in a behaviour change program. The table below highlights some of the differences between anger management and family violence programs.

Table 3: Comparison of anger management and family violence programs

Anger management programs	Family violence programs
Behaviour is often reactive and people have trouble regulating emotions in a wide range of situations.	Problem regulating emotions at home and often impacted by beliefs regarding power, privilege and entitlement.
Explores situations where anger is poorly regulated. Focus on triggers and connections between thoughts, feelings and actions. The context is more often workplace, childrearing and community situations.	Behaviour is often intentional, based on beliefs and involves power/control issues. Includes a wide range of violence – physical, emotional, psychological, financial, sexual etc.
Involves self-esteem, self-care, relationship skills, lifestyle, physiological and emotional issues.	Involves an educational process that explores the use of privilege/entitlement, power/control and equity in relationships. It also involves a therapeutic process to increase the empathy used to understand the impact the violence has on their family.
Can involve mandated clients.	Can involve mandated clients.
Often courses are delivered in a six to 12-week format with a maximum of 12-15 hours.	Often courses are 16-24 weeks with a minimum of 50 hours duration being ideal.
Partners not routinely involved.	Partners are routinely involved and interviewed to ensure they are safe and that change is being sustained.

To ensure a proper assessment is completed, workers should:

- Determine whether the participant has been violence-free for a specified period of time (as determined by your program) and they intentionally commit to changing their behaviour.

- Ensure the participant is able to take full responsibility for his actions.
- Conduct a pre-interview and, if possible, copy court documents or any other referral letters being reviewed.
- Clarify the context where the violence occurred and who was involved. If the issues are experienced in the context of intimate family relationships, the participant should be assessed for the degree of violent/controlling behaviour and referral to a family violence behaviour change program. Be aware that minimising the impact of the behaviour, or denial, is likely to occur.
- Consult their supervisor if any concerns arise that the behaviour is more family violence related. Ensure other family members are safe, and refer the client to a family violence program.
- Support clients who are to be involved in an anger management program, but actually require a family violence behaviour change program. It is important to support the participant by holding them in the existing program until they move into the family violence behaviour change program. A man who is abruptly cut off from a program may feel rejected or humiliated and will be less likely to take up the other referral. All attempts are made to do what is required to ensure safety for the other family members.
- Ensure access to an anger management program is at the determination of the workers and not automatic or merely a right of the client.

While men have a level of emotional awareness, they usually experience and perceive emotions as 'real' and 'natural' and find it harder to engage with ideas of identity and sense of self, and the impact of their feelings. There is a growing awareness of the level of stress for men (and women) in an increasingly demanding society and how this impacts on levels of emotional arousal, frustration, irritability, conflict, anger, etc. This raises the challenge of gender roles, social conditioning, work-life balance, time allocation, etc.

As a result of male social conditioning, many men have learnt to suppress and repress their emotions and are less in touch with their feelings. Since we rely on our own emotional sensitivity to tune into the emotions of others, these men lack understanding of, and empathy towards, their partner's and children's emotional needs. Anger can result from men being unable to process and contain emotional arousal and distress (especially in intimate relationships). To support greater emotional awareness, there is a need to challenge social norms that are reinforced through the media and sport. This issue highlights the importance of role-modelling and education to re-frame masculinity. Men often do not understand the consequences of their expressions of negative emotion, and anger can be a mechanism of power and control within relationships. Many men lack the capacity to reflect and express it verbally, even though it is an important skill. Another key motivator for people to access these programs is by helping parents to develop emotional literacy for their boys.

Men's limitations around emotional awareness are an important issue for effective parenting, and one of the biggest problems is the often heated and hostile issue of separated men's contact with children. Significant evidence now exists regarding the impact conflict has on children. The safety of children and other people is always a fundamental consideration. Some men complete courses and feel they are in control of their anger, but actually still experience significant emotional regulation issues. Men in these groups need to be encouraged to understand that emotional regulation is a lifelong process that continually improves the quality of their life and relationships.

There is a challenge in working with different cultural groups and beliefs about anger management. Some cultures may exhibit behaviour that may appear intimidating/aggressive/abusive to other cultural groups e.g. cultures that readily use gestures, loud voices and strident tones as part of normal communication.

Critical to understanding effective anger management is the use of a process that works with the whole range of emotions in a proactive ongoing way i.e. affect regulation. Workers are required to acknowledge the validity of all emotions right from the start in order to

Andrew King

avoid the suppression, repression and dissociation that cause men to bottle up their feelings, and later blow up, with the use of aggression or possible violence (Sutton, 2007a).

Workers have found it important to use regular check-ins to identify and enable the men to access their feelings. Some tools are valuable, such as the illustrated 'feeling faces' chart that helps men more comprehensively identify emotions. It is important to acknowledge fear as a regular and normal emotion that serves to direct attention towards possible threats in order to maximise survival (physical, emotional and psychological). Neurobiology informs workers on how people are hard-wired by evolution to respond to fear (anger management is fear management). (Sutton, 2007a)

The initial challenge for workers is to develop sufficient trust and initial engagement that allows the men to relax and talk honestly. A variety of useful tools, such as the anger iceberg/volcano, can then be used. The feelings that men might experience needs acknowledgment before working towards identifying and processing underlying issues. It is important for workers to have strong boundaries, be aware of their own emotional issues, and access good debriefing and supervision.

The two key steps for change are for the men to:

- Increase their understanding of their behaviour.
- Consistently find new, non-violent ways of acting.

Useful skills for men to develop include:

- Staying in touch with their own feelings and thoughts when someone is expressing opinions they don't agree with.
- Validating their thoughts, wants, wishes or needs when someone who is important to them has other values and needs they want acknowledged.
- Acknowledging another person's view when he or she holds different opinions, without losing their own integrity.

Bancroft & Silverman's 12-steps to change (2002). The person using family violence must:

1. Disclose fully the history of physical and psychological abuse towards their partner and children.

44

2. Recognise that the behaviour is unacceptable.
3. Recognise that the behaviour was chosen.
4. Recognise and show empathy for the effects of their actions on the partner and children.
5. Identify their pattern of controlling behaviours and attitudes.
6. Develop respectful behaviours and attitudes.
7. Re-evaluate their distorted image of their partner.
8. Make amends in both the short and long term.
9. Accept the consequences of their actions.
10. Commit to not repeating abusive behavior.
11. Accept change as a long-term (lifelong) process.
12. Be willing to be accountable for their actions.

The current approaches being used when working with men and violence are influenced by cognitive behaviour therapy (CBT), narrative counselling, solution-focused counselling and strengths-based practice. Psychoeducational behaviour change programs such as the Duluth Model have been very influential and have contributed to the development of significant tools for change within the cycle of abuse and equality wheels.

Focusing on new skill development and increased understanding of family violence, and even affirming existing strengths, is seen as being more effective in changing behaviour. More recent approaches have the purpose of encouraging men to reflect on 'becoming the man they want to be'. All the approaches discourage viewing the men as having fixed, violent identities.

Some of the core practices for effective interventions:

- Creating a high degree of emotional safety allows for honest disclosure and respectful interaction.
- Working with respect; engaging the group participant as a person who is struggling with and concerned about their use of violence. Avoid thinking of anyone as 'a perpetrator'.
- Engaging the creative rather than the reactive process within men. Discussing reactivity can be non-productive.
- Acknowledging men's stories without condoning behaviour.
- Spending time on what has gone on during the week, which is

often the most useful aspect of the group. This allows the worker to unpack what has happened and the unconscious beliefs that underlie their behaviour. This allows change to occur.

- Shifting the focus onto what men want for their children. It allows men to open up, since they are no longer feeling blamed,
- Being up-front about the limitations of confidentiality. Child protection and the safety of others take priority over confidentiality.
- Validating the positive efforts a man is making. This validation should not collude with any excuses or blaming, but should affirm his intentions to create more respect and care in his relationships.

The worker establishes a 'practice of care' among the men that is missing in many other men's cultures. This care is focused on the safety of key relationships surrounding them and also involves the care of themselves. This is established through supporting attitudes that keep the focus on healthy relationships and equality. It is assumed that men have a core intention of making the world a better place for themselves and their family, and it builds on the motivation of the 'honourable man within' and other honourable intentions e.g. to make a difference, to create a safer world for their children.

Community responses for reducing family violence

Media representations tend to be hugely detrimental to perceptions of men. Men are often represented as disposable or as buffoons. It is possible that this climate can make a man feel quite threatened and even more isolated. Models of masculinity that include competence in the emotional world are needed. Across society, young men need to be empowered to recognise and express emotions.

Workers who work directly with men help to create a safer and more caring society. Working with women is essential for safety and for challenging men's sense of entitlement, but all too often men have been looking for support to change, only to find no services available. This is an ongoing tragedy for Australian communities, for men, women and children. Male-positive counselling practices have to be developed for community agencies. While sensitive work with women continues, men need to have a strong place within community work, taking into account their perspectives and stories. Suggestions to reduce domestic and family violence include:

- Work with men around respectful engagement while holding a focus of responsibility, with the primary focus being on the safety of women and children.

- More trials and evaluation of a broader range of programs that target men's behavior.

- Support for strengths-based approaches and early intervention programs, as well as for community education programs such as the White Ribbon Campaign (www.whiteribbonday.org.au).

- Display posters for Mensline Australia or other specific behaviour change support agencies at local courts throughout Australia to increase access to telephone support services for men involved with family violence issues.

- Avoid single-dimensional views of men. Language such as 'perpetrator' or 'predator' encourages this one-dimensional, deficiency-based view of men. Respectful language will increase the number of men willing to engage with intervention agencies. Use language such as 'users of violence'.

- A focus on the impacts on children when violence occurs in family situations is often the most effective way to engage the parents.

- Use strengths-based approaches that build inclusion right from the beginning of intervention.

- Educate young people to build awareness of the impact of violence in relationships.

Supporting people who experience violence

As part of an early intervention response you will likely speak to the partner who has experienced violence. The following perspectives are useful to consider:

    i.   **Establish rapport and trust.** Rapport and trust require a level of empathy. Empathy, according to Rogers, is 'a way of being with another person' to experience the world of another as if it were our own. Empathy is the central element of the person-centred approach.

To develop empathy, the worker considers questions such as:

- What is the person trying to tell me?
- What does this mean for them?
- How does this person see their situation?

In addition, the worker pays attention to indications of stress and distress, such as slow/fast breathing and stressed words.

    ii.   **Positive reinforcement.** The worker establishes the relationship by providing positive reinforcement to the person for taking the first step to contact. Early in the conversation, the worker will assess the immediate needs and safety of the person. If any risk is present, action may need to be taken to ensure their safety, such as notifying the police or health professionals. Safety is the priority at all times.

    iii.   **Exploration of thoughts, feelings and behaviours.** The worker assists the person in the exploration of thoughts, feelings and behaviours relevant to the problem being talked about, using open and closed questions to clarify and get more information. Questions may include, but not be limited to:

- Are you at home alone?
- Is it safe for you to speak?
- Is the person who is hurting you around?
- Are there children involved?
- Are the children currently safe?
- When did it happen?

- How did you feel at the time?
- Where were you at the time?
- What happened when you said that?

iv. Validation. It is very likely that the person will be afraid and/or angry. The worker validates those feelings and assures them that they (the worker) doesn't take the anger personally.

v. Reflection. Reflecting concentrates on the feelings within a statement and is intrinsically linked with paraphrasing. It captures, in a brief statement, the main points the person has said.

vi. Resource identification. The worker works with the person to identify what they have done to protect themself/children and where they have sought help. It is explained that other services may be useful/appropriate for the current situation.

5. WORKING WITH MEN IN DIFFERENT CONTEXTS

Working with culturally diverse fathers
(King, et al., 2014)

An effective position for community service/health workers when working cross-culturally, and especially with fathers from culturally diverse backgrounds, is to adopt a 'safe uncertainty' approach. This approach attributes equal value to professional expertise and the knowledge and expertise of the client, with regard to their unique situation. It has been described as being in the state of 'informed not-knowing' . That is, workers are never the 'expert', 'right' or in full possession of 'the truth'. A key focus of this approach is to seek understanding rather simply acquire knowledge of the client's situation. When workers are more informed about the life experiences of people from culturally diverse communities, they can become aware of their own cultural biases and then recognise and harness the cultural narratives of the 'other' in a truly strengths-based practice.

A significant component of the engagement process with culturally diverse fathers is for the worker to consider:

- The key issues experienced by the client.
- The underlying impacts of that experience.
- The associated challenges experienced when addressing these issues.

Workers need to be genuinely interested in finding out about the background and experiences of the fathers, and the meaning they attached to those experiences. The extent of how far a worker goes into the client's past depends on the context and nature of the work. The most important message is that workers should adopt an inquiring mindset that is guided by genuine interest in knowing about the client's situation from their point of view. This becomes the medium for drawing out the narrative, providing invaluable validation and normalising the client's experiences.

When fathers from culturally diverse backgrounds come to see workers, they believe that the worker has some expertise that will help alleviate their problem. Workers are more effective when they have already developed some knowledge about their client's culture and gender by engaging in dialogue with colleagues and friends; attending cultural awareness training; watching documentaries; reading books, etc.

Workers are more effective if they have explored, through professional supervision or training, their own socialisation experience and attitudes to achieving culturally sensitive practice. Workers hear the client's story with some knowledge about their background, but not with full possession of 'the truth'. If workers become as informed as possible about themselves and those they perceive as different, they will be able to listen in a way that takes into account cultural biases.

In the case of refugee fathers, it is important to consider the overlap and complex interaction between issues associated with the aftermath of traumatic experiences in the context of organised violence; the problems related to the exile, migration and resettlement processes; and the trials and difficulties that are part and parcel of the normal life cycle (Anderson & Goolishian, 1992).

Many of the refugee fathers who come to Australia experience a significant role change. Through these changes, refugee fathers (like many other fathers) have few opportunities to talk through their concerns with someone else. They respond to issues in the best way they can. Their aspiration to protect their family has to be redefined in Australia because it may have a very different expression than what was culturally appropriate in their country of origin. The new context involves changing feelings about:

- Viewing themselves with honour for being the father or patriarch of their family.

- Identifying who they are in their community and the role they play in the family.
- Revaluing the meaning of their prestige, status and dignity in the family and community.
- Being the main income earner.
- Providing external protection to other family members and keeping them safe.
- Having a clear purpose and role in the family/community.

It is important to talk through the roles and expectations they held before coming to Australia and how these have changed. It is also important to encourage them to remain up-to-date with changes in their country of origin because the sociocultural environment that existed when they left it is often concretised as the normal and ideal set of community values for many years into the future. An example of this is that the attitudes towards women and their freedom in the community may have recently changed in their country of origin. However, people often idealise the values that existed at the time they left as a refugee.

Five important considerations when engaging culturally diverse fathers:

- **Consider the impact of the past experience of their migration to Australia.** Many culturally diverse fathers, whether they are refugees or from refugee-like backgrounds, have experienced some forms of difficulty in their country of origin and migration process. Coming to Australia creates a great sense of hope and the expectation of a better life for themselves and their families. These expectations are not always achieved due to challenges of resettlement in a new country. The impact of unmet expectations can lead to unexplained frustrations, anger and a sense of hopelessness.
- **Work towards building the client's sense of control and safety, and their meaning and purpose in life.** Help them re-establish their dignity and value [and] reconnect them to wider society (Kaplan, 1998). Adopt a curious openness that helps you to understand the client's situation. Be person-centred, but don't probe too much. Let the client. Show

interest and positive regard for them and their background. Be mindful of triggers and the impact of past trauma issues when setting and communicating your role and service. Be transparent and honest, familiarising the client with aspects of confidentiality and privacy, and being upfront about your role.

- **Be aware of how easily the service user can be overwhelmed.** Many newly arrived culturally diverse families easily become overwhelmed by the processes and stresses that settling into a new country involves. At times, a father is quite likely to have a smaller set of relationships or networks to talk through these changes and may appear more isolated or frustrated. Sometimes it may be difficult for parents to provide for basic parenting responsibilities due to the pressures or stress involved. Many of these pressures and stresses on the father centre on obtaining new employment, a change in his potential job role due to a lack of recognition of his original qualification, concern about the future, child/family needs, and worries about overseas issues and responsibilities in his country of origin.

- **Create opportunities to talk about the role changes that have occurred.** The fathers have experienced significant cultural change around ideas and expectations of how their family operates. This includes gender relations, individualism versus collectivism, and extended family contexts versus nuclear families. They may need to learn new skills, such as cooking for the family, because the mother is likely to obtain employment in some situations. This is a new role that may be trivialised by other fathers from their community as it challenges traditional expectations and masculinities, and is seen as a woman's responsibility.

- **Value that the father loves and cares for his children.** Newly arrived culturally diverse families have often undertaken flight or migration in the hope of improving future prospects for their children. Discuss the care of their children:

    o How is this achieved in Australia?

o How do they keep their family safe?

o What is the difference between keeping someone safe and controlling them, or when does it become abusive?

o How do they balance and provide for what their children need?

It is worth stating again that working with culturally diverse fathers is like working with any other fathers. Don't feel that your skills are insufficient or that you are facing an exotic situation beyond your knowledge. The biggest difference is that you have to learn more about their specific past experiences and the impact the experiences may have on their personal situations. Also, workers need a developed sense of self-awareness and self-knowledge with particular focus on understanding their own cultural biases.

Working with Aboriginal and Torres Strait Islander fathers (King, et al., 2014)

To many Aboriginal men, fathering is the most important and challenging commitment in their lives.

Prior to colonisation, Aboriginal people were hunters and gatherers. After colonisation, that identity was gradually eroded in urban Aboriginal people. And yet it is still part of their nature and in their blood. There is still, for some men, a sense of hopelessness, loss and lack of self-esteem. This may not be the case in remote communities where people still live traditionally. But even there, they still have their own unique community challenges.

When working with Aboriginal men, the main thing you need to do is to build up that self-esteem; in a sense, to get that hunting and gathering role back within them. This today means earning a wage, providing for their family and caring for their family. That's what has been lost and why many Indigenous people are in so much trouble today. In many Aboriginal communities, many of the leaders are outspoken women. The Aboriginal men sit back and don't project themselves well. This is now slowly starting to change with the development of Aboriginal men's groups. There is a new excitement and expectation through the work of people in organisations that are working with men. The men are starting to get back their self-esteem, sense of belonging and sense of pride.

The messages for Aboriginal fathers are no different to the messages all fathers need to remember. However, they are more critical and essential for Aboriginal communities due to the social history they have experienced. The following messages need to be reinforced in fliers, resources, programs and chats you have with Aboriginal dads (SNAICC & FAC, 2013):

- **Be there.** Make time with your kids, enjoy just being with them, laughing with them, playing with them and showing them your feelings and love.
- **Be proud.** Respect and be proud of your culture, and let the kids be proud of you.
- **Protect.** Be child-centred, making good decisions for the best interests of your children. Think about how you talk, act and care for them so they grow up safe, happy and proud.
- **Connect.** Be involved with your children at the start and all through their life. Mistakes and challenges will occur, but keep the connection going by letting them know you are there for them.
- **Talk and listen** to your children. Also talk with your kids and to other dads about what it is like being a dad.
- **Feel good.** Mistakes and challenges will occur, but enjoy your kids and enjoy being a dad.
- **The journey.** Think about the lessons you have learnt about life and tell your children and grandchildren about them.

6. Using Generativity to Address Family Violence Issues

"It is human to have a long childhood; it is civilised to have an even longer childhood. Long childhood makes a technical and mental virtuoso out of man, but it also leaves a lifelong residue of emotional immaturity in him." Erik Homburger Erikson (1902-1994)

Erik and Joan Erikson built their stages of human development on a series of dyads, or opposite personality traits. People think of themselves as: optimistic or pessimistic, independent or dependent, emotional or unemotional, adventurous or cautious, leader or follower, aggressive or passive.

Based in part on the study of Sioux Indians on a reservation, Erikson became aware of the massive influence of culture on behaviour and placed more emphasis on the external world, such as depression and wars. He felt the course of development was determined by the interaction of the body (genetic biological programming), mind (psychological) and cultural (ethos) influences. (Harder, 2008)

The Erikson's organised life into eight stages that extend from birth to death (many developmental theories only cover childhood). Since adulthood covers a span of many years, its stages are divided into the experiences of young adults, middle-aged adults and older adults. While the actual ages may vary considerably from one stage to another, the ages seem to be appropriate for the majority of people.

Erikson divided the lifecycle up into eight life stages that are still relevant today and especially relevant when working with men.

Life stages of development
1. Infancy: birth to 18 months
   Trust vs mistrust
   Basic strengths: drive and hope

2. Early childhood: 18 months to 3 years
   Autonomy vs shame
   Basic strengths: self-control, courage and will

3. Play age: 3 to 5 years
   Initiative vs guilt
   Basic strength: purpose

4. School age: 6 to 12 Years
   Industry vs inferiority
   Basic strengths: method and competence

5. Adolescence: 12 to 18 Years
   Identity vs role confusion
   Basic strengths: devotion and fidelity

6. Young adulthood: 18 to 35
   Intimacy and solidarity vs isolation
   Basic strengths: affiliation and love

7. Middle adulthood: 35 to 55 or 65
   Generativity vs self-absorption or stagnation
   Basic strengths: production and care

8. Late adulthood: 55 or 65 to death
   Integrity vs despair
   Basic strengths: wisdom

Central to Erikson's ideas is the belief that, somewhere along the way, the strength of the human spirit can be ignited and deficits overcome. Generativity involves the capacity to care for the next generation and demands the ability to give something of yourself to another person. It includes community building and is historically reflected in the strong support people give to service clubs, Lifeline, SES, Rural Fire Service, etc. Generativity can mean serving as a guide, mentor or coach to younger people or adults. Research indicates that between 30 to 45 years, our need for achievement decreases and our need for influence or community increases. (Vaillant, 2002)

This story outlines how one father put generativity into practice.

David is a father who has not had much meaningful contact with his two sons throughout their 12 years of life. Having experienced a great deal of trauma in his younger years, he has a limited ability to socialise or play with his children. His great desire is to be a better father than his father was to him. He finds this difficult as he has survived intense violence all his life and has resorted to violence many times to deal with any conflict in his adult years. During his participation in the group, David was enduring an ongoing court drama with the NSW Department of Family and Community Services in order to have a meaningful role in the life of his children. The children were being removed from their mother and he was struggling to put a case forward to become their full-time carer. David desperately wanted their life to be better than his own. One of the educational sessions covered a concept outlining the limitations of what we can control, as compared to what we can influence, and letting go of what is outside our control and influence.

David left the program that night enthusiastic about how he could use this idea at his next court date. The following week he returned to the group a very different man: wearing cleaner clothes, holding his body more erect, taking more pride in his appearance and being much happier. He told the story of attending the court the preceding week. The mother of his children had attempted to engage him in a conflict in the court grounds by being verbally abusive and aggressive, and he had refused to engage with her. He had acknowledged to himself that he could not control her, or what she was saying, so he had walked away. This was an achievement.

When the court was sitting, the mother again attempted to engage him in conflict by staring and mouthing swear words at him. He continued to ignore her. When the court proceedings were not going his way and inaccurate information about him was being put forward, he did not react as he had in the past, by trying to use threats and loud language to control the court. Rather, he decided to let it go (as best he could) as he could not control it and instead attempted to influence the court by his 'good' behaviour. Although quite proud of himself for the change in his behaviour in a very stressful situation, the best for David was yet to come.

The case was adjourned. Before he left the court, David approached the solicitor acting for his children and said, "I know you don't like me and that's OK." He then added, "I've been watching and listening to you and you seem like a good person who has the best interests of my sons at heart. I just want to let you know I appreciate what you are trying to do for my boys." The solicitor, in a spontaneous gesture, offered David the opportunity to spend a short time with his eldest son. Not having seen his son in over four weeks, David accepted enthusiastically. He spent 20 minutes with his boy which he otherwise would not have had. David was ecstatic at this good fortune. This generous gesture by the solicitor continues to have a positive impact on David's life because he has experienced the rewards of learning new ways of dealing with conflict.

The generative stage has had more attention and utilisation than the other life stages. It occurs when people focus on the greater impact they have on their immediate world (family, work, community) and their key relationships. The generative approach is still relevant today for both men and women, and especially when working with men. Generativity involves the biological and parental capacity to care for the next generation and demands the ability to give something of yourself to another person.

Generativity is powered by the motivation to "invest one's substance in forms of life and work that will outlive the self". (Vaillant, 2002, p115)

It involves caring for something outside of yourself or taking care of the next generation. The generative fathering framework (Fleming, 2002) is a model for understanding the non-deficit approach to fathering. **Generative fathering** has been described as:

"... fathering that meets the needs of children by working to create and maintain a developing valuable relationship with them." (Hawkins & Dollahite 1997, p18)

Generativity is best understood as a response to the perceived vulnerability of an external situation. While children are often the strongest expression of generativity in people's lives, it has other expressions throughout a lifetime. Some of these other connections are:

- Partner – often minimised when the partner is viewed as being more powerful.
- Service clubs, Lifeline, SES, Rural Fire Service, etc.
- Sport – if your involvement provides rewards beyond the immediate reward of competition and exercise.
- Employment context – if you identify the importance of making a difference in your job.
- Mates (other people you identify with in a similar situation).
- Other key relationships, particularly where vulnerability may exist e.g. a sibling with a disability.
- Wider community interests.
- Dogs/animals/pets.
- Gardening.

"The main concepts in the generative fathering framework are based on two core ideas. The first is that the human context creates needs in the next generation that fathers have an ethical responsibility to meet, and the second is that fathers and their children both benefit and develop from this process of interaction." (Hawkins & Dollahite, 1997, p4, as cited in Fleming, 2007, p16)

Generative fathering involves the next generation and recognises that it is beneficial both to the child and the father. Research indicates that between 30 to 45 years, our need for achievement decreases and our need for influence or impact on some community increases (Vaillant, 2002).

Besides being applied to human development for men, women and fathering, generativity has had a significant contribution to understanding aging. The Harvard Study of Adult Development reviewed societal trends in the last 50 years and concluded that generativity is the best indicator for healthy aging. The study concluded that "the old were put on the earth to nurture the young" (Vaillant, 2002). However, this learning is not about just giving to others, but is also found in the receiving. A matched study (Pagano, Friend, Tonigan, & Stout, 2004) identified that similar generative impacts existed in research about recovery from alcohol addiction using the Alcoholics Anonymous (AA) approach. This research indicated that people thrived most when they invested something of themselves into helping someone else (being a sponsor), independent of how many AA meetings they attended.

Generativity uses the concept of forces where ego strengths are developed through life in response to challenges experienced. The development of strengths (hopes and dreams) and tensions (fears and anxieties) complement other strength-based and resilience approaches that are used today in community services/health practice. When working with men, motivation to change is best mobilised when the focus is not primarily on inner self-reflections but on generative reflections.

Figure 5: How generativity works

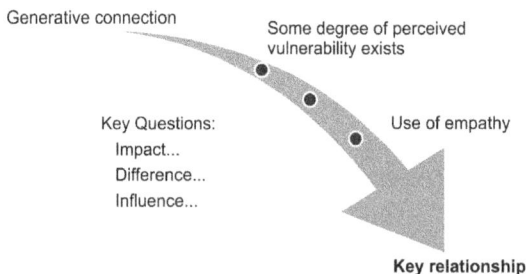

Generative connection

Some degree of perceived vulnerability exists

Key Questions:
Impact...
Difference...
Influence...

Use of empathy

Key relationship

An important insight into generativity is that it is best mobilised when a key relationship has a greater perceived vulnerability than the client themselves. In women's lives, it is better articulated in the ideas of nurturing and mothering, and may be also rejected as a woman stands against these expectations. In men's lives, it is less articulated, which is what makes it more powerful. Often in family violence situations, the men will not see their partner in a generative way (unless they have decided to exploit her vulnerabilities). However, they will often have a generative connection towards their children.

To deepen the generative connection, ask the client questions about the needs of the key relationship (usually focusing on the needs of the child). Focus on the impact the violence has on the relationship and use generative questioning to explore past, present and future insights (see the tools section).

Table 4: Client's response to the perceived vulnerability

Client's response to the perceived vulnerability in the key relationship	
Negative response	The vulnerability and needs experienced in the key relationship is likely to be rejected or even exploited for personal gain
Neutral response	Little attention is given to the vulnerability and needs experienced in the key relationship, with little insight or need for a personal response.
Positive response	There is an interest in and positive response towards the vulnerability and needs experienced in the key relationship.

If the client has a negative response, they offer little to the key relationship and could be quite harmful unless watched. If they have a neutral response, there is opportunity for change and the development of a positive response. If they have a positive response, they have some key strengths that will be useful for the child and help create safety in the situation.

In this story, a father, Tim (fictitious name), uses generativity to make changes in his life:

Tim, aged 38, had to battle with a child protection agency to become the primary carer of his child. Over 12 months, he attended a number of community-based fathering workshops and programs. The agency's psychologist completed two psychological reports in that period, and stated: "In 20 years of clinical experience I have never seen anyone change as much as Tim." Tim's determination and dedication to using these ideas and new learning was apparent to many people.

Just prior to becoming the full-time carer of his child, Tim said: "Taking my daughter home will be the best experience in my whole life. It's like winning the World Cup. Everything else in life has always been taken away from me – that's why I'm paranoid. I have had to learn patience." He also commented on his involvement in the fathers' group: "Thanks for your help. I don't think I would have made it without the group. This group has impacted on me. It speaks about life the way it is. It wasn't pen and paper stuff. My dream has come true. It is achievable if you are determined. A lots of times you can't see the end of the road, but you just have to keep going."

Understanding the generative perspective is useful when working with fathers because it:

- Provides a strength-based framework to understand many men's focus on the external world rather than the internal world of their feelings.
- Emphasises the significance of their relationship with the child that has hopes/ dreams and aspirations for the child regardless of the amount of time they spend with them.
- Values the importance of men seeing that the parenting experience may require greater responsibility that contains a message that you need to often give up something for yourself to gain something.
- Allows you to appreciate the challenge that stepfathers may have to be generative towards the new children in the relationship and not just focus on their connection to the partner.
- Provides a framework of tools to use when working with fathers.

Some generative interventions you could use are:

- Focus on active and practical ways of being in the world and having an influence and impact on others. Use questions that ask about 'impact', 'difference' or 'influence' e.g. "How does your response have an impact on your son?" Discuss how they have an impact, who they influence and who they respect. Also, who are the people who have an impact on, influence and respect them?
- Build on a future focus: how their impact, influence and level of respect with their key relationships will be in the future. Ask "What do you want to do more of?"
- Ask the father to tell the birth story of one of his children. This is a very special opportunity because men usually allow the mother to tell the birth story (as they should). However, by telling their version, they own the experience and the likely changes they face. The birth of a baby is so rich in vulnerability and the need for care that it increases the fathers' ability to connect and attach to the child.
- Challenge perceptions of hopelessness and focus on active responses they still make that look out for or care for other important people in their life. Ask "How do you want to be seen?"
- Acknowledge the challenge of being a reasonable man in an unreasonable situation.
- Discuss clear expectations of how you will work together and what is required, and reduce the fear of the unknown. Identify relationship changes:
  - "What has changed?"
  - "What has not changed?"
  - "What do you want to achieve?"
- Build on discussions that highlight key relationships and the person's significant hopes and fears/anxiety (yearning vs challenges).
- Identify and name key values that are conscious, purposeful and can help to widen the range of choices they can use in response. This identifies and builds on primary motivations.

The generative approach converts the father's anxiety into genuine concern that leads to a commitment to have a positive influence in his child's life. Rather than being a selfless act, it can be seen as adopting a partly self-serving role – investing now to benefit in the future.

A separated father called MensLine Australia and talked about feeling suicidal due to the loss of his children and family. After a 40-minute discussion the man was more stable and no longer feeling suicidal. The counsellor, in summing up, asked: "What was important about this discussion?" The man replied: "Do you know what the most helpful thing was? "While we were talking, I looked down and saw my dog sitting at my feet. I realised that I was still needed to take care of him."

The power of the birth story in mediation

An experienced family law mediator experimented in mediation sessions with the idea of asking both parents to talk about the birth of one of their children and telling each other about their memory. She initially thought clients would say, "You've got to be kidding." The opposite happened. Each parent launched into their story and the other parent started listening. This start to a mediation puts the whole process into a positive framework to begin with. It helps clients to be child and future-focused. It has made a significant change to a high-conflict process.

Challenges to generative connections

These four contexts have an adverse impact on the generative stage:

- Self-absorption.
- Stagnation, depression and other mental health issues (including alcohol/drug dependency).
- 'Generative chill' anxiety (see below).
- Juggling multiple demands.

Self-absorption

When men are too self-focused or self-absorbed, they find it difficult to have empathy for others or respond to other people's needs. Self-absorption may occur due to beliefs about entitlement or a man's emotional responses causing him to primarily focus on his own needs being met.

Stagnation, depression and other mental health issues

Mental health and/or addiction problems have a significant effect on men's motivation to be involved in support services. Some fathers drop out of a group due to these issues. Others use the experience as part of their change program. In order to meet the challenge of supporting a participant's recovery, programs need to be flexible enough to allow longer-term involvement. Alcohol or drug misuse often skews a person's perception of their needs and what response is required in a certain situation.

Peter is a young stepfather with a dependence on marijuana. One week he said: *"I gave up pot for three days, but I have had a challenging week. I'm trying to do the right things, but no-one gives me any credit."* He talked about the challenge of the family and the social context he lives in: *"I want to say 'f... it' and leave. But the love you have stops you. The kids really love me.* "*It's been my life. I smoke a few cones (marijuana), drink beer and watch TV. I can't get a job as I need to learn to cope first with hassles at home. Dad overdosed last year. Since then, things have gone downhill."* He went on to talk about the daily battle he has regarding his choices: *"I don't want to walk out of the front door because the neighbours will say, 'Come and have a smoke.'"* After four months, Peter still resisted seeing a drug and alcohol counsellor and he recently left his relationship. This is the tragedy that often impacts on families where there are addiction issues. It is important for programs to be able to work simultaneously with recovery, relationship and child protection issues.

Generative chill

Extreme threats to an adult's parental generativity can cause 'generative chill', a type of anxiety resulting from a perceived or real danger of losing the child or children they have helped to create (Snarey, 1993). It is likely that brief or extended threats to generativity will have a significant impact on a father's selfhood (Snarey, 1993: p87). Family breakdown presents separated fathers with a threat that often results in depression.

Generative chill (Hawkins & Dollahite, 1997) is a useful concept for understanding how fathers disengage from their children. The challenge is how men can rebuild this generative connection. Professionals and close family members may want to help men deal with the pain of their family separation, but it is the father's timing alone that will ultimately dictate when he is open to rebuilding connection, engagement or reunion with his child.

Generative chill (Hawkins & Dollahite, 1997) is described as the anxious awareness people experience arising from the threatened loss of the relationship with one's child. The reaction men have to family separation will be influenced by how they deal with this experience. When separation is managed well, generative chill is a motivation that creates a stronger father/child relationship. When separation is managed poorly, generative chill becomes depression, despair and disengagement. The generative fathering framework is a non-deficit approach to fathering that supports a process for rebuilding engagement. It is vital that separated fathers value the new roles they play in their children's lives. The primary roles that fathers have played in the family before the family separation occurred may need to be re-adjusted e.g. providing financial security or being the protector (while this role may not exist in reality, it still provides a high level of motivation for men). Secondary roles that traditionally may have had less prominence, such as cooking for the children, reading stories and talking about ordinary life experiences, will become more important and rewarding in the new post-separation relationship.

While the reassessment of these roles will be difficult, the new roles used post-separation are often more rewarding and relationship-enriching. The following case is an example of this reassessment of a new role:

Mike (fictitious name) is a separated father in his early 40s who came very close to throwing himself in front of a train due to depression. The relationship problems in his life and lack of contact with his children were a continual struggle for him. He was often overwhelmed by the depression and his inability to change his post separation parenting situation. He eventually attended a father's group and spoke about it being a vital place where he could be himself regardless of how the week had gone.

He stated: "It has been a good 12 months. I have received good support that has helped me to keep sane while I battle to see my son. Attending the group has turned around my whole relationship with my older son. I still play the memory game with my boy and he loves it. I feel a lot closer emotionally to him and understand why he reacts that way too." He added: "The kids are my main priority. I now accept that Sue and I have finished our relationship. I am sleeping a lot better now." He changed his employment and moved to a new area, and he values all the child contact opportunities that are possible.

Juggling multiple demands

Men and women alike often juggle a variety of roles and pressures in the normal course of the day. Men, however, may not choose to demonstrate generative responses due to many barriers such as work time constraints and the stress experienced as a result. The best response to review the balance of life's demands is to be transparent about the available choices and possible consequences. Professionals may then discuss with men the alternative choices they can have and those with the best possible outcomes can be selected.

Applying generativity to different groups of men

Men's health campaigns and relationship programs work more effectively and attract wider interest when they build on generative connections in men's lives. Here's a list of how generative connections can be used with separated fathers and fathers in general (King and Fletcher, 2009, p42):

- Find out the man's preferred name and introduce yourself.
- Find out how many children he has, their age and their special interests.
- Build a connection around how your work context is relevant to him and the context of his children (remember, he is unlikely to express a need for support and help).
- Assume, and discuss with him how it shows in his responses, that he has the desire and the ability to:
  - Commit - the physical and ongoing support a father provides and his awareness and involvement with a child throughout their lifetime.
  - Choose - the capacity to make day to day decisions for the children that meet their needs.
  - Care - the ability to attend to the important transitions in a child's life and provide the optimal conditions that maximise their growth.
  - Change - the ability to adapt as children grow older and the father matures in his relationship with the children.
  - Create - the creation of resources for material comfort and the resolution of problems to allow opportunities for the development of emotional wellbeing.
  - Connect - the ability to form lasting and healthy attachments with a child. These will change over time to meet the child's evolving needs.
  - Communicate - the capacity to relate with children by sharing meaningfully with them, verbally and non-verbally.
- Discover the man's way of expressing his connection with the children (using the above abilities).
- Explore opposites or tensions – what helps/blocks and what is valuable or a distraction to achieving the above.
- Normalise experiences he has and validate the strengths men bring to parenting.
- Amplify the significance of positive choices he makes in his child's life.
- Discuss what the role of fathering means today. What parts of the role are important to him?

- Build the metaphor of walking alongside him in the work you do. Find out how this may be helpful to him rather than telling him what to do.

If appropriate, ask some of the following questions. Beginning with, for example: "I would like to find out about some of your experiences with your child (who is called Sam) and what those experiences mean to you and Sam."

- "Can you tell me about the most enjoyable experience you ever had with Sam? What meaning does that experience have for you now?"
- "Can you tell me about an experience when you felt especially close emotionally to Sam? What meaning does that experience have for you now?"
- "Can you tell me about an experience when you cared for and nurtured Sam? What did you learn about nurturing children from that experience?"
- "Can you tell me about an experience when you felt especially distant emotionally from Sam when he/she needed you to be there for him/her? What meaning does that experience have for you now?
- "What was the most painful experience you ever had with Sam? What meaning does that experience have for you now?"
- "Are there any particular things that help you to be the kind of father to Sam that he/she needs you to be?"
- "Are there any particular things that prevent you from being the kind of father to Sam that he/she needs you to be?"
- "Can you tell me about any important sacrifices you have made in your life that demonstrate how much you care about Sam?"

If relevant, it may also be useful to ask:

- "Who or how do you protect others in your life?"
- "Who do you keep safe?"
- "What happens when the protection of others is misused?"
- "What is the difference between keeping someone safe and controlling them?"
- "When does protecting someone become abusive?"
- "How do you keep yourself safe?"

Separated fathers

- Find out the man's preferred name and introduce yourself.
- Find out how many children he has, their ages, when separation occurred, what orders are in place and when he last had contact with his children.
- Build a child focused connection as central to your relationship with him.
- Build on language that values respect, 'being a reasonable man', 'maintaining integrity', providing what your children need (emphasising safety, security and connection). Until proven otherwise, believe that he has a shared interest in these values.
- Acknowledge and normalise feelings if he sees himself being treated unfairly as a father and reaffirm the importance of how fathers are seen today.
- Build a strong metaphor of walking with him in the work you do. Find out how this may be helpful to him (using perceived equality) for guidance.
- Explore what he can control in his situation, what he can influence and what he can't control or influence. Relate this to specific examples in his life.
- Affirm the importance of showing respect for the children's mother, regardless of what has happened, because the children love her and will benefit from seeing this from their father. This is central to the father respect he seeks to have attributed to him.
- Explore the importance of timing – not being too impatient and also appreciating the positive aspects of what may already exist in times spent with his children.
- Support him to tune into the feelings and needs of his children and what is required to help make his life safe (abiding by any court orders), nurturing and valuing (towards key relationships in his life).
- Encourage him to keep a diary and live the values that are important to him and his children. If his friends have children, encourage him to maintain some interest and understand how quickly children develop and change.

Fathers who have rebuilt engagement with their children have identified a number of useful steps:

- Maintain a journal over several months to monitor progress.
- Obtain current information about the children.
- List one's own positive strengths that are core to personal values.
- Identify a professional support person or mentor.
- Access a mediation service through a family relationship centre.
- Write a list of the key lessons they have learnt through their life.
- Prepare for reconnecting with the children slowly, without having firm expectations of what will occur. Remember to be openly responsive and supportive to the children no matter what reaction they may have.
- Show positive regard for the child's mother. It's not good enough to not mention her to the children.

This reflective story, from a case worker at a family relationship centre, has a strong theme of generativity:

During a psycho-educational group for fathers, I identified this man, Charlie (fictitious name), who seemed pretty angry with his wife, Clare (fictitious name). Charlie was in the military. He had a young family and was separated from his wife. He spoke of Clare failing to understand the importance of his role in the military. He made reference to the three young Australian soldiers killed last year in Afghanistan. He became righteous in his tone when he spoke of how they gave their life fighting for their country. Charlie demonstrated a strong sense of patriotism and camaraderie for his fallen countrymen. His conviction was strong. He explained that he, too, was going overseas and appeared quite proud of that fact.

As Charlie spoke of his relationship with Clare and their children, there seemed to be a disconnection from them. He spoke angrily of Clare, stating that she controlled when he saw the kids, that she was "screwed up", and that she didn't understand the importance of his role. Clare was the target of his blame. I acknowledged the importance of his role in the military. I asked him what he meant by insisting that Clare didn't understand his role. He said she wanted him to "get out" and that was the source of much of their arguments. I suggested that it made him angry because Clare seemed to have misunderstood his intentions and the importance of his role in the family. He agreed.

I explored what was going on with Clare and Charlie. I suggested to Charlie that his wife might be scared of losing a husband and the father of her children by his serving in a combat zone. I asked if he had discussed her fears with her and found he hadn't. I directed the topic to loyalty and patriotism. I said the patriotism he had for his country was admirable, but asked about his patriotism to his family. "I'm not sure what you mean," he replied. I explained that Clare was perhaps fearful of him being killed in combat and that this was very real for her as there were constant reminders on the television and internet and in newspapers. I added, "You are very patriotic to your country, but there is also patriotism, loyalty and honour owed to your family. They look at you to keep them safe and secure, and Clare is fearful if you're thousands of kilometres away in some foreign country with God knows what going on. Step into her shoes!" He didn't respond. Later I discussed the matter with my colleague to find out what he thought. We considered Charlie was an angry man and we felt we hadn't managed to get through to him. Charlie gave positive feedback in the evaluation form, but as for putting things into practice, we were doubtful.

A few weeks later, I was doing a telephone intake. As I spoke with the woman, she revealed that her co-parent had changed since coming to the centre. She reported a side she had never seen before in the several years they had been together. She told me he was not acting in anger and was spending more time with the children and with her. She told me they were even considering reconciliation. She said they were talking and discussing things really well. I looked down at the file and recognised the name. It was Clare. She was talking about Charlie. I asked her, "So in all the years you have been together, have you ever seen him like this before?" "No," she said. I asked her how she felt. She said she liked it and spoke of what a good man he had become. She said, "Before he would get very angry with me and the kids and yell, but now we talk!"

7. Using a Generative Approach to Work with Tensions

In 1995, the Western Australian government's Family and Domestic Violence Taskforce developed a non-punitive campaign called Freedom from Fear. It primarily focused on men who have used violence (or showed potential to use it), asking them to seek help to change their violent ways (Donovan Research, 1996). The logic behind the campaign was that if violent men voluntarily changed their violent behaviour, it would not only reduce the incidence of violence, but also reduce the fear felt by their female partners and children. After extensive interview testing among men who use family violence, they chose to use a child-focused approach that explored the impact of family violence and supported men to access local behaviour change services. In 2008 this initiative was success-fully replicated at Hull in the United Kingdom.

Focus group and individual interviews were used to develop the most effective approach. They found that the theme of criminal sanctions, community intervention and social disapproval had little impact in the testing stage. The theme of *damage to partner* was not seen as a key motivation by men who had used violence. This theme was dismissed as likely to be ineffective. However, in contrast, the *effect on and damage to children* was universally seen as a very powerful notion among men who had used violence:

- All expressed strong feelings for their kids (while very few expressed any feelings of fondness for their partners).
- Their children's reactions to specific instances of domestic violence had a very vivid impact on many men who had used violence.

- Many of the younger men who had used violence could relate to their own feelings when they were kids, and some talked about how domestic violence had affected them as children. Thus, this theme had relevance whether or not they themselves had children.

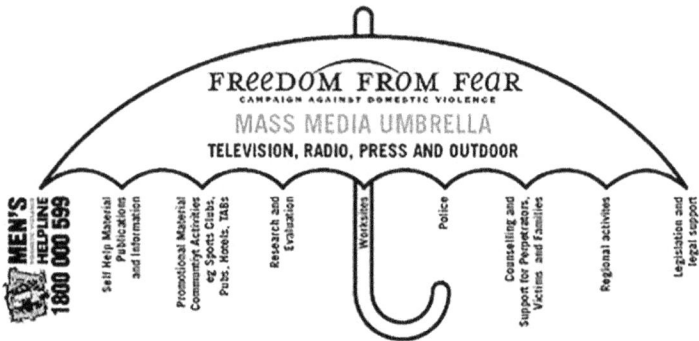

Figure 6: Overview of Freedom from Fear Campaign

Very little research has focused directly on the characteristics of violent men as fathers. Usually men are viewed as rigid and authoritative (Bancroft & Silverman, 2002), uninvolved in their children's lives and negligent of their basic needs (including those thwarted by the violence). A more complex picture of violent men as fathers was portrayed by Fox and her colleagues (Fox & Benson, 2004). A qualitative study on the fathering of eight men who participated in MBC groups found that the men expressed feelings of guilt, shame, remorse and responsibility regarding the damage they caused as fathers and wished to fix it. The authors point at the potential contribution of the men's fathering role to their sense of self, which in turn may lead to a less defensive inspection of their abusive behaviours and an increased motivation to access further support. Below are the images used in the Freedom from Fear campaign in Hull, England. (Stanley, 2009)

Figure 7: Images from the UK Freedom from Fear campaign

Focusing on the tension of generativity

It is a cornerstone of behaviour change work to not work with men who use violence if the harm they have inflicted on their partners and children remains unacknowledged. Perel and Peled (2008) chose to relate to the violent men as simultaneously vulnerable and harmful. They avoided a one-dimensional focus on problems and weaknesses by identifying existing strengths. They adopted a warm, empathic, respectful, appreciative attitude towards the interviewees, and they avoided criticism as much as possible.

Building on the generative perspective, the study identified how positive attitudes lay at the core of the men's perceptions of fathering in general and of their own fathering in particular. They viewed fathering as one of the most important domains of life, if not the most important, and themselves as good fathers. This is a significant motivation of behaviour change and is already used in a variety of programs.

There is often an unspoken tension in many men between the **yearning** to be a good dad and the individual **challenge**, and the impact this has on their children:

- To "live for your child".
- To "give your kids everything and be the best possible dad".
- To "be a good dad"

and the tension of

- Exposing the children to violence
- How family violence impacts on their children
- Being the controller
- Being an absent dad

Overall, the violent men Perel and Peled (2008) interviewed presented themselves as good fathers. The images of 'the good father' they constructed seemed to combine their ideal perception of fathering and of themselves, and the reality of their lives.

"To give him everything and be the best possible dad."

Throughout the interviews, they noticed various ways the men used to construct their image as good fathers. These included providing material needs, protection, education and creating a warm connection with the children. In the spirit of traditional conceptions of fathering, the breadwinner or provider roles took precedence over the other attributes of good fathering. When using generativity, this hope and aspiration is acknowledged, along with the fear or challenge that the threat of violence creates.

Perel and Peled interviewed fathers who expressed strong reactions towards the impact violence had on their children. The aim of generative discussions is to link the significance of past/present/

future reflections that acknowledge these tensions that, unanimously, leave fathers with a strong yearning for connection with their children and that their violence is a significant threat:

"I was less than a good father, I would call it a bad father, because it passes on a kind of trauma to the child." (Freedom from Fear MBC group)

"All the blows, he saw all these things, all the shouting, all the quarrels, all these not nice things. He absorbed it. Listen, this child is already soaked to the skin, excuse me, in this shit, and it's not appropriate." (Freedom from Fear MBC group)

"I think if you saw your children cowering or hiding, or even flinching from you, because they thought you were going to hit them, I think that would be a really big wakeup call… certainly more so than [if you saw] your wife or partner cowering in a corner." (Freedom from Fear general public focus group)

"It petrified me as a child, and the one thing I don't want to do is make my child see me as a monster… I have shouted at my wife and I've seen the look on my son's face." (Freedom from Fear BME focus group)

"And that, that will stay with me forever… just that look on his face. A mixture of disgust and terror, and I think just the fact that a 12-year-old saw what I was doing was just probably hardest thing to bear." (Freedom from Fear MBC group)

The yearning for a close and warm relationship with the children was displayed in many of Perel and Peled's interviews. This yearning, often unattainable, played a central role in the drama of the interviewees' fathering. The drama was intensified by the clash between the men's image of 'the good father' who maintained a warm relationship with his children and the processes of tension as described above.

The key steps in working the generative tensions:

What is a key relationship that has greater vulnerability than himself?

Discuss the significant hopes and dreams for that relationship	*Discuss the fears and anxieties for that relationship. Name the threats.*

Discuss important issues using relevance, faith building and honesty/directness.

Discuss what choices exist that enable him to strengthen this key generative connection.

Perel and Peled's (2008) findings tell the story of fathering of men who were violent towards their partners. The men's basic attitude to fathering was positive. It was perceived as being of the utmost importance, the men devoted considerable efforts to being a 'good father' as they perceived it, and they felt they were indeed good fathers. Their aspirations, however, were undermined by internal and external forces that included:

- Their own childhoods
- Their personal limitations
- The children's exposure to violence
- The experience of co-parenting

The violence sets off a process of constriction, accompanied by feelings of frustration and yearning, through the father's controlling and violent presence in the home; by accelerating separation, divorce or disconnection from the home; and by further damaging the adult relationship. The quality of the adult relationship is a major factor affecting the quality of fathering. Fathers tend to withdraw from their children when in conflict with the mother.

Implementing a child-focused approach

- Bring children's stories into the program – their experiences of family violence and how it affects them. Bring and use the adult's reflections as a child.
- Use perspectives of being a child/parent.
- Pose the question, "How would you feel as a child watching family violence occur between your parents?"
- Explore reflections of their childhood – ask the men to write a letter to their fathers; use discussion about what they missed from their fathers and what they would like as fathers/future fathers.
- Promote empathy building – that the child's needs are greater and more vulnerable than their own.
- Focus on men's strengths, their love for their children.
- Set up activities groups for fathers and children.
- Use positive images that are displayed on the fridge.
- Ask, "Will your child be able to come to you in the hard and difficult times?"

Building cooperation with men

- Establish confidentiality.
- Create a safe environment (for individuals and the group).
- Support the development of trust.
- Use direct language.
- Use homework to encourage integration with the rest of their life.
- Avoid asking about feelings; use the sharing of stories and "What impact did that have?"
- Reframe old patterns or behaviours and look for exceptions.
- Use goal and boundary setting.
- Encourage accountability and ownership of the change process.
- Encourage responsibility – use solution-focused approaches.
- Encourage transparency – it reduces suspicion.
- Refer the men to a behaviour change group.
- Give permission for men to be honest.
- Engage the men regarding issues, and brainstorm their ideas.
- Develop new tools to deal with their anger by being more empathic and assertive.

8. Using Safety Plans with People Who Use Violence

Useful assessment screening tool (Johnston, Roseby, & Kuehnle, 2009)

Assess the family violence pattern using the following criteria:

1. Potency of violence – level of threat, need for immediate protective orders, likely to escalate.
2. Pattern of violence – degree of traumatic stress, potential for future violence, need for longer-term restraints on abuser, best predictor for future violence, can include casual and contributing factors.
3. Primary aggressor violence - rather than an illusion of it being mutually or jointly instigated there is a person who has previously used violence more often than their partner.
4. Parenting problems – managing children's behaviours and maintaining appropriate limits.
5. Perspective of child – can identify that the child is more vulnerable than they are.

The safety plan is focused on maximising safety while balancing responsibilities. Although family violence is a very important factor to consider when making parenting or safety plans, the capacities of people who use violence and those who experience it are likely to vary greatly depending on the nature of the violence. Other than providing clinical descriptive criteria, tools to reliably differentiate between types of violence and how they might relate to parenting are still in their infancy.

Five basic factors should be considered (Jaffe, Johnston, Crooks, & Bala, 2008)

- Potency of violence
- Pattern of violence
- Primary aggressor violence
- Parenting problems
- Father's perspective of the child/children

See the table (Jaffe, Johnston, Crooks & Bala, 2008) at the rear of this manual for an outline of considerations for what may be allowed in the safety plan regarding contact with the child by the parent who uses violence:

- Co-parenting
- Parallel parenting
- Supervised exchange
- Supervised contact
- Suspended contact

Potency of violence

The degree of severity, dangerousness and potential risk of serious injury and lethality is the foremost dimension that needs to be assessed and monitored so that protective orders can be issued and other immediate safety measures taken and maintained. Prior incidents of severe abuse and injuries inflicted on victims are an important indicator of the capacity of an individual to explode or escalate to dangerous levels. In some cases, explosive or deadly violence can erupt with little or no history of abuse, but other warning signs are often evident.

Pattern of violence

The extent to which the violence is part of a pattern of coercive control and domination (rather than a relatively isolated incident) is a crucial indicator of the extent of stress and trauma the child and family suffer, and the potential for future violence. It also suggests what kind of protective, corrective and rehabilitative measures to take (e.g. high-security supervision of visits, substance abuse or psychiatric treatment). The pattern of violence is the best predictor of future violence and helps you to understand the degree of traumatic stress, potential for future violence and the need for longer-term restraints on the abuser.

Primary aggressor violence

Assess whether there is a primary aggressor of the violence (rather than it being mutually instigated or initiated by one or the other party on different occasions). This will indicate whose contact needs to be restricted. Accounts of the violent incident(s) by the participants themselves should be assessed with caution because victims may tend to assume more blame, and abusers usually minimise or deny their conduct. Moreover, the motivation to conceal or admit violent behaviour varies depending on the aggressor's views of the consequences of doing so (e.g. he is unlikely to admit abusive behaviour to a court, but may do so in an appropriate therapeutic intervention). Nevertheless, it is helpful to obtain a detailed account of the violent incidents, within the context of the relationship, from each party separately.

Identifying the predominate aggressor red flags (Roberts, 2016)

- Presents as overly charming and charismatic.
- Seems overly calm and confident, has no fear or apprehension about the incident –a civil or criminal response that might result.
- Refers to his partner in aggressively critical or demeaning terms as a character attack or out of righteous anger rather than fear based anger or anger about the violence.
- Discusses the incident in vague and general terms rather than providing specifics.
- Describes events or circumstances that are inconsistent with the known facts.
- Reports facts that are inconsistent with his size or that of his partner.
- Has injuries that are more consistent with him being the aggressor and which are different to the injuries sustained by his partner.
- Conveys through his use of language, a sense of ownership, entitlement, privilege, jealousy or obsession about his partner.
- Is critical and opinionated about ways that the system responds to family violence –i.e. Courts, Police.

- Focuses on his rights and how he feels they are being violated.
- Appears to regard his children as his property, believes they need to show him respect and be taught a lesson and appears to be unable to focus on his children's needs.

Parenting problems

How are the family violence issues reflected in the child's behaviour? What safety plan needs to be in place to ensure the best care and support for the children?

Fathers' perspective of the children

Does the father appreciate the vulnerability of his child or children? Is he clearly able to appreciate his child's vulnerability as needs that are separate to his own need to be right, validated or get his own way?

Does that insight impact on how he responds to the family violence issues?

Useful questions to ask:

- Who do you protect in your life and how do you protect them?
- Who do you keep safe?
- What happens when the protection of others is misused?
- What is the difference between keeping someone safe and controlling them?
- When does protecting someone become abusive?
- How do you keep yourself safe?

CAUTION

Workers need to be wary of differentiating the abuser from the victim based on who claims to be the victim; who is more charming, charismatic and likeable; who appears more organised, reasonable and sensible; and who feels more entitled and morally outraged. Sociopaths, narcissists and chauvinists who use violence for interpersonal control can make a very smooth presentation, whereas the victim can appear emotionally distraught and disorganised.

Table: Proposed Parenting Plans in High Conflict and Violent Separating and Divorced Families (adapted)

Jaffe, P., Johnston, J., Crooks, C., & Bala, N. (2008). Custody disputes involving allegations of domestic violence: Toward a differentiated approach to parenting plans. Family Court Review, Vol 46. No. 3. 500-522.

Section A: CO-PARENTING	Access arrangements	Other provisions	Appropriate for	Not appropriate for

• Shared decision-making on major issues—education, health, etc. Common child care practices, consistent routines, discipline expected across homes
• Ongoing communication & joint problem solving by parents
• May be called joint legal & joint physical custody.
	• Time share ranges with specific provisions stipulated in court order or by agreement of the parties
	• Explicit court access order includes holidays: explicit dates, times, places of exchange
	• Flexibility & compromise re schedule are encouraged, where possible
	• Court order provides back-up when no agreement is reached about any temporary changes negotiated by parents directly.
		• If requested by either party, permanent court order, such as restrictions on taking child out of area w/o consent, etc. Protocols for telephone access to child
		• Comfortable place of exchange for both parents & child
		• Protocols for communicating emergency information.
			• Parents sufficiently able to communicate, have measure of trust in & respect for one another; able to be child focused or able to resolve difficulties
			• Re DV: Low ratings on potency, pattern, & primary perpetrator of violence, e.g.,
			  ◦ Low levels of Separation induced
			  ◦ Violence [SIV] after crisis is passed & trauma resolved
			  ◦ Other types of past violence, only with substantial history of successful parallel parenting & cessation of abuse & control
			• Some mentally ill & substance abusers with substantial proof of rehabilitation
			• High level of recognition of the violence and its impact on the child.
				• Cases with DV in general Chronic conflict, coercive interactions, inability to joint problem solve, no history or capacity to cooperate & communicate
				• Mentally ill & substance abusers in general.

Table cont.

Section B: PARALLEL-PARENTING	Access arrangements	Other provisions	Appropriate for	Not appropriate for

• Divided decision-making responsibilities, different issues allotted to each parent
• Parenting plan provides for clear boundaries & separation between parents
• Time-share schedule requires minimal communication, seeks to avoid direct parent-parent contact, and also provide stability & continuity in child's life
• May be joint or sole legal & physical contact (if joint, the time-share schedule should meet all the above criteria).
	• Unsupervised day &/or overnight visits for VP
	• Time sharing between parents may range, as specified by the court
	• Natural transition times & places minimize disruption of child's school, social, & extra-curricular activities
	• Explicit court order for access (times, dates, place of exchange, holidays, etc.)
	• Expect adherence to details of court order (not flexibility & compromise re changes)
	• Consistent, safe child-care practices within separate homes are emphasized rather than common practices.
		• Protocols in place to avoid conflict, threat of any violence, & sabotage between parents
		• Permanent restraining orders in place
		• Restraints from taking child out of area w/o consent
		• Neutral place of exchange— safe & comfortable for child (e.g., neutral relative, contact centre, school, library)
		• Structured telephone access to child
		• Rules in place for communicating emergency information between parents
		• Other necessary info communicated by email, etc. (never by child)
		• Procedure in place for resolving any new issues, e.g., parenting coordinator.
			• Each parent has a positive contribution to make in time spent with children, but direct parent-parent contact provokes acrimony
			• Chronically conflicted non-violent couples (incl. repeated unfounded DV allegations)
			• Re DV: Moderate-low ratings on potency, & pattern, no primary perpetrator, e.g.,
			  ◦ Conflict-instigated violence [CIV]
			  ◦ Separation-induced violence [SIV] during & post-crisis
			  ◦ Other types (incl. abusive relationships with credible evidence of good progress &/or, completion of appropriate programs)
			  ◦ Victims traumatized by past violence of any type (incl. VR), but no longer a threat
			• Some level of recognition of the violence and its impact on the child.
				• Infants & very young children, & special needs children who require consistent & closely coordinated care across family homes
				• Child experiences ongoing symptoms of trauma & distress
				• Findings that one parent poses a physical, sexual, or emotional threat of abuse to child
				• Any on-going threat of violence to one parent by the other.

Table cont.

Section C: SUPERVISED EXCHANGE	Access arrangements	Other provisions	Appropriate for	Not appropriate for

• Decision-making authority & parenting time assigned solely to the parent more able to provide a non-violent home
• Time-share schedule requires minimal communication, seeks to avoid direct parent-parent contact, and also provide stability & continuity in child's life
• Usually involves sole legal residency & limited physical contact.
	• Monitored exchange between parents
	• Transfer of child by third party at neutral site to buffer child & prevent ongoing conflict at transitions
	• Exchange supervisor monitors behaviour of all parties, enforces rules, & helps communicate essential information
	• Access usually limited to several hours or day visits, but may have overnights
	• Explicit court order for contact (times, dates, place of exchange, holidays, etc.)
		• Specific goals & behavioural criteria that need to be met for VP to graduate to non-monitored exchange
		• Explicit court orders in place detailing exchange arrangements (all times, dates, location, monitors)
		• Safety provisions for victim parent & child in place, e.g., escort to site, protective orders in place
		• Permissible activities & persons allowed / not allowed during visits (optional)
		• Restraints from taking child out of area w/o consent
		• Rules in place for behavioural etiquette at time of exchange, & permission for any attendance at child activities.
			• Re DV: Moderate ratings on potency, pattern, & primary perpetrator of violence where risk or fear of renewed violence or conflict occurs only when parents meet, e.g.,
			  ○ Conflict-instigated violence [CIV]
			  ○ Violent Resistors [VR] & other victims with residual trauma from past violence
			  ○ Separation-instigated [SIV] during crisis period
			  ○ Other types (incl. abusive relationships with credible evidence of good progress &/or, completion of appropriate programs
			• Chronically conflicted non-violent couples (incl. repeated unfounded allegations)
			• Problematic behaviour or distress at transition by either parent &/ or child needs checking
			• Some level of recognition of the violence and its impact on the child.
				• Any current threat of violence and ongoing concerns about safety & wellbeing of child with either parent alone
				• Inadequate monitoring or non-neutral monitor.

Table cont.

Section D: SUPERVISED CONTACT	Access arrangements	Other provisions	Appropriate for	Not appropriate for
• Decision-making authority & parenting time assigned by court to the parent more able to provide non-violent home • Usually involves sole legal residency & limited physical contact.	• Supervised Visits for VP • Supervised in a safe place with a neutral supervisor who agrees to terms of a detailed supervision order and is able to control the VP and willing to report violations to court • Explicit court order for access (times, dates, place of exchange, supervisor, etc.) • Duration of visits usually limited to a few hours.	• Specific goals & behavioural criteria that need to be met to graduate to monitored exchange • Safety provisions for victim parent & child in place, e.g., escort to site, protective orders in place • Support & treatment services offered, but victims (& violent resistors) empowered by respecting self-determination • Court-ordered program attendance/rehab for person who uses violence.	• Re DV: High ratings on potency alone & moderate-high ratings on potency, pattern, & primary perpetrator of violence: ○ Currently or recently violent (all types of violence) ○ Abusive relationships • Current substance abusers & acutely mentally ill, if treatment in progress • Temporarily for ambiguous cases during a DV assessment • Parents with established risk of child physical, sexual abuse, abduction threat to child • Child may have been traumatized by DV or abuse, but wants contact or stands to gain from parent's continuing involvement.	• Child's ongoing distress & lack of any apparent benefit in contact • Inadequate supervision available, i.e., lacks training, skills, not neutral for child or parents • Child or visiting parent needs more intensive therapeutic intervention • Visiting parent has met explicit conditions for less restrictive contact • Custodial parent remains distrustful & wants supervision despite unfounded abuse allegations following full assessment.

Table cont.

Section E: SUSPENDED CONTACT	Access arrangements	Other provisions	Appropriate for	Not appropriate for

• Decision-making authority & parenting time assigned by court to the parent more able to provide non-violent home
• Usually involves sole legal residency & limited physical contact.
	• All access or visiting rights with VP are suspended as per specific court order
	• May resume after court review for specified period of times, contingent on specific remedial behaviours being reliably demonstrated.
		• Report critical incidents to child protection services
		• Referral of case to child protection services if suspension is expected to be long term or permanent
		• Specify goals & behavioural criteria that need to be met to graduate to supervised access.
			• No meaningful parent-child contact seems possible: no remorse or willingness to change by abusive parent
			• Persistent distress or refusal of child to supervised visits
			• Parent's (VP) non-compliance with terms of supervised contact order
			• Re DV: Very high ratings on potency, pattern, & primary perpetrator, e.g., abusive VP's with:
			  ○ Attempts or threats to abduct, seriously hurt, kill, or blatant use of child to hurt & harass other parent
			  ○ Conviction for serious assault or attempted homicide or homicide of family member
			  ○ Child completely estranged from parent &/or family due to trauma of past abuse by VP
			• Some severe current substance abusers & acutely mentally ill (no treatment).
				• Supervised visitation is not conveniently available
				• Custodial parent's (CP) unjustified refusal to make child available for supervised visits or other non-compliance with terms of order.

9. Tools and Exercises When Working with Men Who Use Violence

1. Word tools to focus and deepen discussions

Family Violence

This is a useful tool for further exploring situations where the violence is recognised and acknowledged. The purpose is *not to shame the person*, but to allow the client to develop insight and understanding about the power of these words. Write a single word or phrase (e.g. safety, anger, violence) on a piece of paper and place it on the floor or table. Looking downwards enhances the reflectiveness. This is a powerful way to focus a discussion and consider a subject from a variety of angles.

This tool uses the principle of externalisation. Discussions are likely to go twice as long, and twice as deep, when they are externalised. Through externalising, clients experience themselves as having wisdom, insight, understanding and agency. Due to the multisensory focus, it is very like solution-focused counselling (on steroids).

Useful questions include:

- How does this word affect you?

- How does this word affect other people in your life?
- What feelings go along with this word?
- How long has this word had a significant impact on your life?
- What are some different ways of dealing with (the word)?

Ask them to think about their life if their issue was removed. What would this be like? What would be different? You may want to replace a word with a strengths-based/positive word such as 'safety'. Place this paper on top of the original word and discuss the difference.

Link the discussion to the value gained through the person accessing local behaviour change services.

Reflect on how you would use this tool in your workshop scenario:

_____

_____

_____

_____

_____

2. Crossing the line

|⌞_____|_____⌟|

Caring   Controlling   Abusive

Context: The roles of being a 'protector' and 'provider' have a traditional impact on many men. Most men value some expression of these roles, but rarely discuss how they make decisions about appropriate responses. These roles are equally shared with women. It is the assumptions in these situations that encourage inappropriate choices and incubate abusive actions. The most important wisdom in life affirms that the decision to keep others safe needs to be negotiated with and agreed to by all parties, otherwise the protection starts crossing the line of control because it reflects only the man's insights and needs.

When to use: This exercise is used when working with men to deepen their understanding about the decision to protect others (or be caring towards) and when this becomes abusive or controlling. The worker's own self-reflection is valuable for modelling insight and providing wider perspectives.

Conducting the exercise:

Paper version

On a sheet of A4 of paper, draw a line across the page and mark three positions. Write the word 'caring' in the left-hand position. Discuss what this word means in their situation. Then write 'controlling' in the middle and discuss what this word means in their situation. Then write 'abusive' at the other end and discuss what this word means in their situation. Give examples of what each position looks like as a behaviour.

Movement version

Alternatively, doing a physical version of this exercise whilst standing can be very useful for some clients. Ask the client to stand up after you have discussed a situation they faced in their family. Using a continuum, highlight three different positions – being protective; being controlling; being abusive. Give examples of what each position looks like as a behaviour.

Points to highlight:

- Being caring, supporting, protective – these actions can be useful and honourable, but they ***need to be negotiated and not assumed***.
- Being controlled – less useful in relationships; not against the law, but viewed as unhealthy and an indicator of many other problems.
- Being abusive – an act of violence; against the law and very problematic.

Discuss what protecting others means. How they keep others safe and when it crosses the line to being abusive. Ask these questions:

- Who do you protect or keep safe in your life?
- How do you protect or keep others safe in your life?
- What happens when the protection of others is misused?
- What is the difference between keeping someone safe and controlling them?

- When does protecting someone become abusive?
- How do you keep yourself safe?

Extension questions:

- Revisit the situation and ask them, "when the situation occurred (that you have been discussing) in what position was the intention of your behaviour (being a protector; controlling or abusive)?
- If we asked other key people in your life (e.g. the partner, their children), what position was their behaviour (being a protector; controlling or abusive)? If necessary, ask...
  o Where would your children place your behaviour?
  o Where would the mother place your behaviour, and the police, and other key people?
- What can you do to change your behaviour to be less controlling or abusive?

Link the discussion to the value gained through the person accessing local behaviour change services.

Reflect on how you would use this tool in your workshop scenario:

———————————————————————

———————————————————————

———————————————————————

———————————————————————

———————————————————————

3. The control, influence and letting go circle

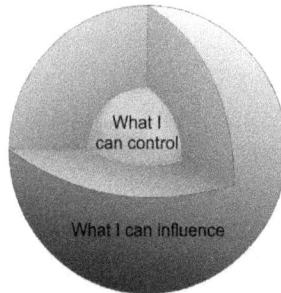

What I cannot control or influence - Let it go!

Context: This is an excellent exercise for reviewing a situation and accepting what can be controlled and influenced, and what needs to be let go of.

What can be controlled in life is in fact a small, very limited area. Anyone can control only what they wear, where they go, who they spend time with and their own behaviour. **People do not have the right to control others!**

The larger circle is the area of influence. It is larger than the area of control, but still limited. Conflict in life is increased when people try to control what they can only influence, or attempt to influence what is outside their control or influence. When attempting to control a situation, or a person who is outside their influence and control, people have no choice but to use power. A person must force others to do what they want. This force is violence.

This misguided attempted to control issues in life often occurs in family separation, when separated fathers are in conflict with the mother of their children. Unless the children are in potential or actual danger, each parent has the right to attempt persuasion and to influence the other parent, and no right to try to force their view of 'how things should be' on the other. If it is not going the way they want, they need to learn how to 'let it go'.

Outside the larger ovoid shape write 'outside our area of influence and control'. There are now three distinct areas:

    o Our area of control

o Our area of influence

o Outside our control <u>and</u> Influence

It is of paramount importance to the wellbeing of relationships and ourselves that people clearly differentiate between these three areas. Often the most important issues in someone's life are out of their control or influence. Conflict or violence results when one party attempts to control these things.

To attempt to control a situation, or someone who is outside someone's control and influence, they must use some type of force or power:

- Physical force – violence or the threat of it.
- Intimidation – creating fear.
- Humiliation.
- Threats to do something or withdraw love and attention.
- Force of will.

The more power/force used, the greater the conflict and feelings of mistrust. Although challenging, people must learn to let go of what is outside of the areas of control and influence. A simple thing to say, but in reality, a very challenging thing to do.

When to use: This exercise is used when working with men to improve cooperative ways to respond to situations. Men often overestimate the amount they can control situations and issues.

Conducting the exercise: Ask the man to think about an issue or concern. Draw two circles (or ovals) using the same centre. A smallish circle in the centre, with a larger circle on the outside. There should be a wide space left on the outside of the circles before the edge of the paper.

What I cannot control or influence - Let it go!

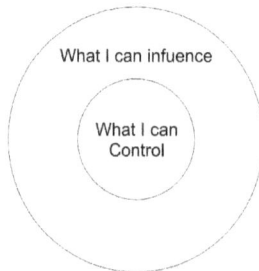

What I can infuence

What I can Control

Together, discuss and write down the things they can control in the situation (the answers should refer only to themselves; their feelings, actions, thoughts – "I" or "my", etc). Then, thinking of the same situation, write down all the things they can influence, but can't control. It may be necessary to define 'influence': you can have some impact, but the ultimate outcome is unknown. In the outside area write down all the things they can't control or influence. They need to let go of these things because they can't have an impact on them. Write the words 'Let it go' and discuss how this may be achieved. It doesn't mean that they aren't important.

The skill involved with letting go doesn't mean forgetting or ignoring. Some letting-go techniques:

- Focus on your control of your breathing.
- Acknowledge feelings, but don't treat them as a fact.
- Acknowledge the important values and goals decided upon previously.
- Remember and hold on to significant connections in your life.

Discuss what is learnt.

Extension questions:

- What situations in life do you misjudge the balance of control/influence and letting go?
- How do you let go of issues you feel strongly about?

Link the discussion to the value gained through the person accessing local behaviour change services.

Reflect on how you would use this tool in your workshop scenario:

_____

_____

_____

_____

_____

4. Cola bottle exercise

Context: This exercise is useful to explore anger, conflict, violence and the role of beliefs.

Take a bottle of cola out of your bag, shake it. Ask the client to open the bottle. They are very likely to decline. Ask them why? They will say that they don't want cola all over the place. Tell them that the cola bottle is like our anger and conflict. It's like the problem with violence. When we quickly take the lid off, it creates a mess that someone else has to clean up. Discuss who the people are who clean up the mess violence creates.

This introduction is critical because it highlights that anyone using abuse and violence is capable and competent to change; that the use of any violence (taking the lid off and letting it rip) **is always a choice**.

Extension questions:

- Ask them to hold the bottle and reflect on how it symbolises their emotions. Talk about a few examples that fit the metaphor.
- Discuss how anger is a secondary emotion (the fizz at the top) while the other primary emotions are the black mass beneath. Talk about what their primary emotions are and how the metaphor of a black mass enables us to understand that feelings are often difficult to identify. Value the importance of the black mass of feelings within the individual.
- Sometimes the most dangerous bottles are those that show no foam/fizz, but other people live in fear of them exploding. It strips the other people of their confidence and ability to predict.
- Discuss how they can respond to this in their actions.

- Discuss the concept of Timeout Part 1: Put the cola bottle on the ground and discuss the concept of time out where you let it have some space to settle. A lot of men fully understand this concept. Emphasise the problem of combining timeout with alcohol, as in it being similar to putting a lollie in a cola bottle. Lollies increase the explosive reaction by 16 times.
- Now discuss the challenge of doing Timeout Part 2: Pick up the cola bottle and highlight that, when it has settled, you need to come back and slowly take the lid off to share it with someone who is important to you. As is encouraged in many soft drink advertisements. This is also a very big challenge for many men to do. It is likely to be when you feel your vulnerability the most.
- Discuss how their beliefs about the other person influence their behaviour. Identify as many beliefs as possible that they have about women. Reality check them and challenge them as required.
- Put the bottle back on the floor and highlight that their children are like little cola bottles, but they have very weak lids. Discuss the challenge of how they can help their children to learn self-control and keep their lid on. This involves them making many mistakes...

Link the discussion to the value gained through the person accessing local behaviour change services.

Reflect on how you would use this tool in your workshop scenario:

---

5. Anger iceberg (with consequences)

When you express these responses, the consequences and impact on relationships are..
- Pushes people away
- Decreases safety
- Decreases trust
- Decreases closeness
- Increases distance

Angry
Rage Fury
Frustration
Annoyance Resentment Irritation
Helpless Powerless
Fear Out of Control Stressed
Drained Depleted Discarded Empty
Hurt Pain Loss of Confidence
Sad Worthless Anxiety Loss of Confidence Incompetent
Loss of Self Worth Put Down Unwanted Criticised
Pulled in many Directions Rejected
Traumatised
Betrayed Used
Abused

When you express these feelings, the consequences and impact on relationships are..
- Draws people closer
- Increases safety
- Increases trust
- Increases closeness
- Decreases distance

Context: This exercise is used to deepen a person's understanding of situations that involve anger, the range of feelings experienced and its consequence.

When to use: When working with men to deepen understanding about situations, anger and its consequence in their life.

Conducting the exercise: Ask the man to complete the short sentence, "I felt angry when…." e.g. "I felt angry when Tom ignored me and didn't do what I asked."

Recognise and briefly discuss these points:

- Anger is neutral. It is just one of the emotions people experience.
- The expression of anger can be destructive or constructive. People mainly experience anger as a negative event. From experience, anger is often scary, abusive and intimidating.
- Anger is a normal emotion and it needs to be regulated/managed and expressed appropriately.
- It is often the people we love the most who receive the full force of our anger and suffer accordingly.

On paper, draw the outline of an iceberg as illustrated below.

Ask the person for words that describe what you would have seen them doing when the situation occurred. These are words that describe what other people would see when they are angry. Write these words on the visible tip of the iceberg. For example:

- Angry
- Pushing the person
- Rage
- Punching walls

- Yelling
- Frustration
- Resentment

Emphasise that anger is a secondary emotion. Other, more vulnerable feelings sit below the surface of the iceberg and are primary emotions, which continue to drive the anger when it is not resolved.

Examples of other feeling words that fill the underwater part of the iceberg:

- Fear
- Helpless
- Powerless
- Out of control
- Drained
- Depleted
- Empty
- Stressed
- Hurt
- Pain
- Pulled in many directions
- Impotence
- Worthless
- Anxiety
- Put down
- Incompetent
- Loss of self-worth
- Loss of confidence
- Sadness
- Lonely
- Rejected
- Unwanted
- Criticised
- Judged
- Misrepresented
- Betrayed
- Abused
- Used
- Discarded
- Traumatised

When people are able to name the feelings, they create a stronger connection that strengthens their ability to respond positively to anger.

Through expanding their vocabulary in describing the feeling world, people are likely to increase their level of intimacy, closeness, safety, and trust in their important relationships. This is a significant discovery for many men because feelings are often separated from actions and consequences, and may be minimised. This exercise highlights the direct connection between how we respond to our feelings and the ultimate consequence that occurs.

After discussing the iceberg and the insights gained, highlight by writing in a small box above the water the consequences of expressing anger inappropriately with those who are most loved or closest to us (write these words to the side of the iceberg). Say: "I want to show you something very important. When you only show the world the actions above the surface, it…" (write down some of the following consequences):

- Pushes people away
- Decreases safety
- Decreases trust
- Decreases closeness
- Increases distance
- Increases fear in the relationship

Then highlight the consequences of expressing the other primary feelings that occur below the waterline. After some silence, and time to discuss reflections about the above, say: "But when you share some of the feelings below the surface by expressing the primary feelings, it…" (write down some of the following consequences):

- Draws people in
- Increases safety
- Increases trust
- Increases closeness
- Decreases distance
- Decreases fear in the relationship

An example of the anger iceberg:

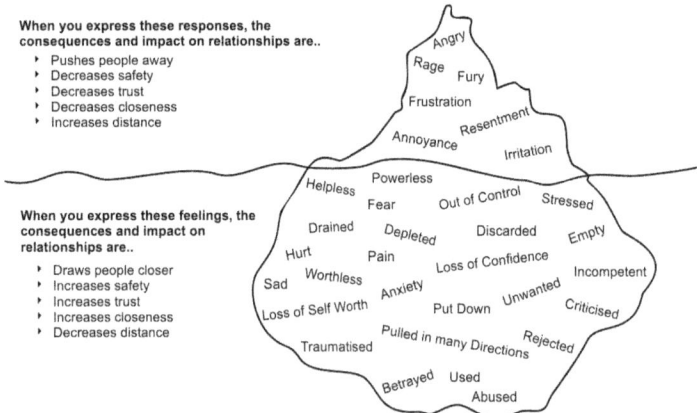

After the iceberg is filled with feeling words, ask the person to pick up the sheets they completed earlier in the session, finishing the sentence "I felt angry when…." Ask them to cross out the word *angry* and replace it with another feeling word; whatever other feelings they were experiencing at that time. The words may or may not be located under the surface in the anger iceberg.

Once this is complete, ask them to read aloud what they have written. After they have done this, use empathy skills to suggest a few more feelings they may have experienced. This will help broaden their understanding.

This concept can be used in everyday life:

- The iceberg allows people to name the feelings that occur in their own inner world. Naming feelings enables people to have a wider emotional vocabulary and rely less on anger. This skill takes time to learn, and patience is needed until the new skill is mastered.

- The iceberg is a very useful way for people to learn about empathy. As they become more familiar with their own inner world and feelings, they can teach their children to use the skill when they express themselves.

Extension questions:

- What impact does your anger have on key relationships around you?
- What difference would occur if you chose to focus on and express the feelings beneath the surface of the iceberg?
- What difference would other people (your children) notice about you?
- What impact does the expression of the underlying feelings have on your relationships?

Link the discussion to the value gained through the person accessing local behaviour change services.

Reflect on how you would use this tool in your workshop scenario:

_____

_____

_____

_____

_____

6. Challenging the victim role

Context: When working with men, it is important to challenge perceptions of hopelessness and the victim worldview. Men's behaviour is often more dangerous (towards themselves or others) when these perspectives substantially exist. These perspectives are best challenged by recognising the importance of making choices and valuing our response, even if it means being reasonable in an unreasonable situation.

When to use: This exercise is used when working with men to deepen their understanding about situations and their own victim or survivor response.

Conducting the exercise: Using the Life Story Cards for Men (free download from http://groupworksolutions.com.au/downloads), ask the men to select a card that reminds them of a time in their life when they felt helpless or a victim to life's circumstances (not necessarily a victim to violence). Then select a card that presents them as a survivor, where they stood against a great difficulty, even if it was only a small but significant response.

Acknowledge the challenge of being a reasonable man in an unreasonable situation. Ask them to discuss what they learnt from recalling these two different stories.

Extension questions:

- In both stories, ask how do you want to be seen?
- In both stories, what was a life-preserving response they used? What impact did it have on others around them?
- What have they learnt about being a survivor? Who did they learn these survivor skills from?
- How do they help their children to learn survivor skills?

Link the discussion to the value gained through the person accessing local behaviour change services.

Reflect on how you would use this tool in your workshop scenario:

_____

_____

_____

_____

_____

7. Generative perspective questioning

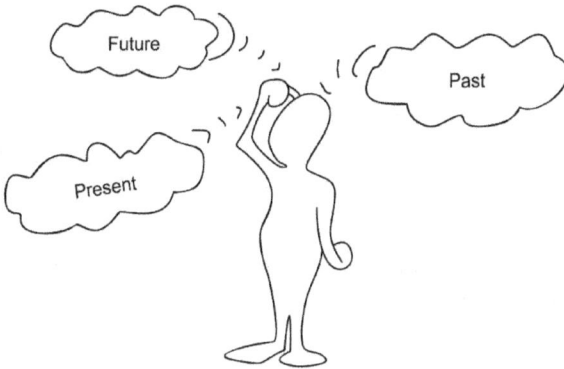

Generative perspective questioning uses key words such as influence, impact, responses, respond, value, respect, significant hopes/dreams – challenges to explore people's focus on three dimensions:

- Past
- Present
- Future

The questions use the principle of triangularisation, meaning that their full effect occurs when people consider their response to a question from each dimension. Here are sample questions for each dimension:

Examples of generative perspective questions – focus on **past** context

- When you were growing up, how did your parents treat each other?
- How were you disciplined as a child?
- How would you describe your childhood?
- How did you feel when your parents fought?
- What impact did your parents' relationship have on you?
- Did you see your mum and dad as good role models?
- How did you see your mother in your life as a kid?
- What stands out about your father when you were a kid?
- What is your strongest memory of your father while growing up? What stood out most?
- What influenced you most about your father? What stood out?
- How do you perceive your childhood?
- Tell me about a happy time you had with your parents growing up as a child.
- Did you attend the birth of your children? What was it like?
- How did you feel when your children were born? What hopes and aspirations did you have for them?
- What did you do when your parents got angry?
- What were the happiest times when you grew up?
- When your mum and dad fought, and your dad used physical violence, what was it like for you to witness these incidents?
- How was it when you grew up?
- What was your relationship like with your child/dad?

Examples of generative perspective questions – focus on **present** context

- How did your child sleep after the incident happened?
- (Child's name) is really important to you! How do you think she/he's feeling right now?
- Do you know what your child (name) was doing when you were throwing the plates at the wall?
- How does this impact on your child?
- How would your child describe you?
- How would you feel as a child watching family violence occur between you and your partner?

- How would your 5-year old (age of their child) describe what they see?
- How would your 5-year old (age of their child) describe your actions?
- Do you scare yourself or them?
- How does your child react?
- If your child could see you at those moments, how would they be feeling? What expression on their face would you see?
- If this incident happened to your mate and his child, what you would think about that?
- How would your child describe you?
- When the incident happened, what was it like for your child?
- How do you think this affects your child?
- How do you think your child sees you?
- What do you think your child would say about you?
- What's the best thing your child would say about you now?

Examples of generative perspective questions – focus on **future** context

- What type of parent would you like your children to be?
- What can you see yourself doing with your children in 10 years' time?
- How do you think increased father involvement in your children's life when there is low/no conflict has positive impacts on all areas of their development?
- What common interest do you want to develop to build the relationship with your child?
- What sort of relationship would you like to have with your grandchildren?
- What sort of relationship would you like your son to have with his kids when he has a family?
- What is one quality you would like your grandchildren to remember about you? What steps would you need to take to make that happen?
- Choose a picture from the set of Men's Life Story Cards (free download from http://groupworksolutions.com.au/downloads) to represent where you would like to be as a parent in three months' time.

Link the discussion to the value gained through the person accessing local behaviour change services.

Reflect on how you would use this tool in your workshop scenario:

Generative questioning

Past	*Present*	*Future*

8. Developing generative connections questions

Discussions that use deeper generative questions are important, especially when applied to important life issues (such as violence). Complete the table below to have a framework that deepens the impact of generative connections. The last part of the discussion identifies the choices a client may use and the consequences (likely result) for those options.

What is a key relationship that has greater vulnerability than himself?

Significant hopes and dreams for that relationship.

Reactive fears and anxieties for that relationship. Name the threats.

Important issues to discuss using relevance, faith building and honesty/directness.

What choices need to be explored that enable him to strengthen this key generative connection?

Link the discussion to the value gained through the person accessing local behaviour change services.

Reflect on how you would use this tool in your workshop scenario:

_____

_____

_____

_____

_____

9. Using ANEC to manage conflict

Often it is hard to know what to say in conflict situations. ANEC is a good tool to remember.

A	**Acknowledge that a conflict is occurring.** Until conflict is acknowledged, it runs the risk of exploding. A simple acknowledgement often reduces some of the pressure surrounding conflict and allows an opportunity for greater learning or change to occur. A lot of energy in conflict situations simmers because people feel they haven't been fully understood. When conflict occurs, the worker needs to acknowledge the issue and the importance of that issue for the client. Try using the statement, "This is an important issue…".
N	**Normalise the feelings involved in the conflict (not the actions, behaviours or responses).** Conflict usually involves intense feelings where someone judges themselves or someone else due to what was said or done. Normalising allows participants to see conflict as a common and normal life experience that allows relationships an opportunity to develop. Emphasise that the importance is on how the conflict is dealt with. This reduces the intensity of the feelings involved and allows the issue to be examined with less emotion. When the conflict occurs between a small number of group members (2-3 people), link its relevance and importance to the other group members and the wider community. This systemic approach to viewing conflict normalises the experience of conflict to being an issue that most people continually learn about. For example, with two parents arguing about different approaches to discipline in a parenting group, demonstrate something about how this discussion is occurring throughout the wider community among many other parents.

E	**Explore the issue as appropriate.** Exploring the conflict involves understanding the foreground and the background of what is occurring. In a group, it involves allowing the participants directly involved an opportunity to express themselves, as well as inviting observations from others involved. At all times, blame and intellectualisation is avoided or challenged by the worker. Avoid blaming or scapegoating any client, and if this occurs, return to acknowledging the issue and normalising the feelings. The worker may decide that, due to the issues being too different from the context of the program, they will meet with the people concerned after the session has ended to discuss the issue further.
C	**Choices about how to deal with the conflict.** When sufficient exploration has occurred, a decision needs to be made about how to deal with the conflict. These choices need to be clearly understood and the relevant parties need to take responsibility for what they decide. As a result of the discussion, identify what needs to happen next. These choices may involve: • The development of a new understanding of each other and the issues. • An agreement that people will 'agree to disagree'. • A plan to continue to discuss the issue at another time. • Clearer ways of working together to achieve a common purpose.

10. Safety plans

Safety plans (used with a person who uses violence) are similar to the plan used with the person who has experienced the violence. In high-conflict situations, it may be better to not show the other parent the plan unless required.

Using the person's insight, explore their understanding of what is happening and the importance of safety. Discuss threats to the safety and how they can best respond.

Use the contact tables in chapter 8 to ensure the considerations are sound for what is allowed in the safety plan regarding contact with the child by the parent who uses violence:

- Co-parenting
- Parallel parenting
- Supervised exchange
- Supervised contact
- Suspended contact

Five basic factors should be considered :

1. Potency of violence
2. Pattern of violence
3. Primary aggressor of the violence
4. Parenting problems
5. Fathers' perspective of the child or children

Link the discussion to the value gained through the person accessing local behaviour change services.

Reflect on how you would use this tool in your workshop scenario:

Safety plan template

Situation of likely concern	Past/Present behaviours to be avoided	Alternative behaviours to be used	New beliefs/ values to be observed

REFERENCES

ABS. (2013, December 11). Personal Safety, Australia, 2012. Retrieved from Australian Bureau of Statistics: http://www.abs.gov.au/ausstats/abs@.nsf/Lookup/4906.0Chapter7002012

Anderson, H., & Goolishian, H. (1992). The service user is the expert: A not-knowing approach to therapy. In S. McNamee, & K. Gergen, Therapy as Social Construction. London: Sage.

Bancroft, L., & Silverman, J. (2002). The Batterer as Parent: Addressing the Impact of Domestic Violence on Family Dynamics. Thousand Oaks, CA: Sage.

Cooke, T. (2006). Engagement . NSW MBC Network Conference. Sydney: NSW Men's behaviour Change Network.

DeKeseredy, W., & Dragiewicz, M. (2007). Understanding the complexities of feminist perspectives on woman abuse: A commentary on Donald G. Dutton's Rethinking on Violence against Women. Violence against Women August 2007 13, 874-884. doi:10.1177/1077801207304806

Dobash, R., & Dobash, R. (2004). Women's violence to men in intimate relationships. The British Journal of Criminology, May; 44, 3.

Dutton, D. (2006). Thinking outside the box: Gender and court mandated therapy. In J. Hamel, & T. Nicholls, Family Interventions in Domestic Violence. New York: Springer.

Fleming, J. (2002). Just the two of us: The involvement of fathers in building stronger families. Developing Practice; Winter.

Flood, F. (2006). Violence against women and men in Australia: what the Personal Safety Survey can and can't tell us. DVIRC Quarterly; Edition 4; Summer.

Fox, G., & Benson, M. (2004). Violent men, bad dads? Fathering profiles of men involved in intimate partner violence. In R. Day, & M. Lamb, Conceptualizing and measuring father involvement. Mahwah, New Jersey: Lawrence Erlbaum Associates Publishers.

GCDVIP. (2014, March 1). Gold Coast Domestic Violence Gold Coast Risk Assessment Tool. Gold Coast, Queensland, Australia: Domestic Violence Prevention Centre, Gold Coast Inc .

Harder, A. (2008). Learning Place Online. Retrieved from The Developmental Stages of Erik Erikson: http://www.learningplaceonline.com/stages/organize/Erikson.htm

Hawkins, A., & Dollahite, D. (1997). Generative fathering: Beyond deficit perspectives. California: Sage Publications.

Heise, L. (1998). Violence against women: An integrated ecological framework. Violence against women, Vol 4. No.3. June, 262-290.

Jacobs, E., & Schimmel, C. (2013). Impact Therapy - The courage to counsel. Star City, WV: Impact Therapy Associates.

Jaffe, P., Johnston, J., Crooks, C., & Bala, N. (2008). Jaffe, P., Johnston, J., Crooks, C., & Bala, N. (2008). Custody disputes involving allegations of domestic violence: Toward a differentiated approach to parenting plans. Family Court Review Vol 46. No. 3, 500-552.

Jenkins, A. (1993). Invitations to responsibility. Adelaide: Dulwich Centre Publications.

Jenkins, A. (2009). Becoming Ethical. Dorset, UK: Rusell House Publishing Ltd.

Johnson, M. (2007). A General' Theory of Intimate Partner Violence: A Working Paper. Retrieved from Michael P. Johnson: www.personal.psu.edu/mpj

Johnston, J., Roseby, V., & Kuehnle, K. (2009). : In the Name of the Child – A Developmental Approach to Understanding. Michigan: The Free Press.

Kaplan, I. (1998). Rebuilding Shattered Lives. Melbourne: Victorian Foundation for Survivors of Torture.

King, A. (2005). The 'quiet revolution' amongst men: Developing the practice of working with men in family relationships. Children Australia, Vol. 30, No. 2, 33-37.

King, A., Fleming, J., Hughes, D., Dukluy, M., Daley, M., & Welsh, R. (2014). Men's Health Resource Kit – Kit 3: Practitioner's Guide to Men and Their Roles as Fathers. Penrith: MHIRC, University of Western Sydney.

Mulroney, J. (2002). Women's Domestic Violence Court Assistance Program Support Workers' Kit. Sydney: Women's Domestic Violence Court Assistance Program Training and Resource Unit.

Pagano, M., Friend, K., Tonigan, S., & Stout, R. (2004). Helping other alcoholics in Alcoholics Anonymous and drinking outcomes: Findings from project MATCH. Journal of studies on alcohol, 766-773.

Pease, B. (2008). Engaging men in Men's Violence Prevention: Exploring the Tensions, Dilemmas and Possibilities. Sydney: Australian Domestic and Family Violence Clearinghouse. Issues Paper 17, August.

Perel, G., & Peled, E. (2008). The fathering of violent men: Constriction and yearning. Violence against women Journal Vol.14 No. 4 April .

Roberts, D. (2016, May 14). Working with men who use family violence -Safely. Melbourne, Victoria, Australia.

Slade, A. (2006). Reflective Parenting Programs: Theory and Development. Psychoanalytic Inquiry, 26(4), 640¬-647.

SNAICC, & FAC. (2013, January 21). SNAICC resources. Retrieved from You're a dad: http://www.melmailing.com.au/snaicc/modules/orders/SNAICC%20resources%20order%20form%20V6%20Nov%202012%20copy.pdf

Sonkin, J. (2008). Defining Psychological Maltreatment in Domestic Violence Perpetrator Treatment Programs: Multiple Perspectives. Under submission to The Journal of Emotional Abuse.

Stanley, N. (2009). Men's Talk: Tackling Domestic Violence. Summary of the presentation (pp. 1-32). Cardith: Gender and Child Welfare Network.

Sutton, S. (2007a). Putting the baby back in the bath; reintegrating psychology back into work with DV perpetrators (unpublished paper). National Men's Health Conference. Adelaide: AMHF.

Sutton, S. (2007b). Pitstop Anger Workshop Manual–Revised 2007. Sydney: Centacare.

Turnell, A., & Edwards, S. (1999). Signs of Safety: A Solution and Safety Oriented Approach to Child Protection Casework. New York: Norton.

Vaillant, G. (2002). Ageing Well. New York: Brown and Company.

Wade, A. (2015). Response-Based Work with Men who have committed Violence. CatholicCare. Sydney, Australia (pp. 1-27). Duncan: Centre for Response-Based Practice.